The Ma
Money & Tax

Helen Monaghan

**MICRO
BOOKWORM**

Published in 2019 by Micro Bookworm

Copyright © Helen Monaghan

Helen Monaghan has asserted her right to be identified as the author
of this Work in accordance with the Copyright, Designs
and Patents Act 1988

ISBN Paperback: 978-1-9161863-0-9
Ebook: 978-1-9161863-1-6

Any interpretations of what is claimable is at your own discretion
AND you must always get the advice of an accountant or HMRC
before taking any action or claiming something extraordinary.

Published with the help of Indie Authors World
www.indieauthorsworld.com

IndieAuthors
World

To Sarah Knight

I quote Sarah from your book *Get your Sh** Together (1st edition):*

"maybe you can write a book about how to file your taxes like a goddamn adult and I'll be the first in line to buy it".

Here it is Sarah, and for everyone else out there too.

Reviews

"You would think that a book with "tax" in the title would be dry and difficult to read. Well, unbelievably, Helen has managed to write it in such a chatty style that it is easy to read, very accessible, and dare I say, even enjoyable! Importantly, it also covers four main areas which are exceptionally helpful if you are self-employed. First, helping you acknowledge and overcome any resistance you have to understanding your finances, tax and tax returns. Second, some practical solutions to finding time which were very well explained. Third, what you need to know and do to complete your tax return, broken down into short, simple steps. And finally, the bigger picture – how all of this helps you become more successful financially and why you should feel good about paying lots of tax. This was certainly a shift of mindset for me and a powerful perspective."

Anna Davies, Achieve Balance

"This book is a superb read for those looking to file their tax return with ease. It is so refreshing to have a book about tax returns that is simply laid out and easy to understand. Helen writes in a wonderfully calming manner and adds lots of humour along the way which inclines you to keep reading and gives you lots of confidence that you can take control of your finances. However, she doesn't disguise the seriousness of the tax system so the reader is left in no doubt about the work that they have to do! The examples and case studies are really

helpful and useful in helping the reader understand how their business is standing from a financial point of view. I would highly recommend this book to all business owners who are either new to tax returns or those looking for a refresh and to check in with their business."

Charly Anderson, Business Owner & Lead Drama Practitioner, Love Drama

"I found the early parts of the book about my mindset familiar. As a coach myself I am only too aware of these things - but do I do them myself - well no and that is the issue! I realise I need to tell myself that I can do this type of work and that I will get it into my poor accountants on time - why am I adding to their stress and mine by continually doing what does not work and leaving to the last moment. I love the bits which say - if you are a computer person do this, if you are not and prefer paper do this - love it. So I get to choose the method and don't beat myself up about the fact I 'should' be better on the computer than I am. When I came to the piece about getting brown envelopes I thought - well I sort of do this already in a slightly different format but I ignored that voice and went off and got the envelopes anyway and without angst, calmly noticing that it is helping me recall and act on things I need to do. I like the explanations about why i.e. understanding the tax man thinking and useful questions to ask, especially 'Did this purchase add to your business or not?' It's a great question. That will really help me as I am someone who needs to know why in order to do it! Onward and back to my brown envelopes - enjoying the order that brings to my mind and calms me down making me feel in control."

Margaret Wright, Individual & Organisational Consultant

"From the moment I started reading I felt that this book was aimed at me, each of the chapters addressed a problem which I have and I literally couldn't believe it. My first thought was that I would be ashamed for people to know how disorganised/last minute I have been with my finances, but this book helped me see that I am not alone. I actually knew that but it was still validating and more importantly motivated me to change. I feel that I can change and I am changing. I found myself writing notes as I was reading and going back over the spreadsheets. I do feel guilt and shame about ticking all the boxes (i.e. that each chapter seems to describe me exactly) and I yearn to be the business owner who needed help for her first two tax returns and now does it herself. I do have a lot of fear about tax, and specifically of getting it wrong. I also started dreaming about a life devoid of money worries. Overall I found this book incredibly helpful and inspiring because I feel that I actually can do it. I also love the way that psychology is weaved into the book as I totally connect with that."

Jen Wood, Coach, Psychotherapist and Consultant.

Contents

Introduction   9

Chapter 1- Overcoming the distractions   15

Chapter 2 - I'm useless at doing my accounts   23

Chapter 3 - Where do I find the time?   30

Chapter 4 - Everything is a priority!   46

Chapter 5 - Everyone else does theirs last minute   63

Chapter 6 - Not knowing where to start   70

Chapter 7 - Fear of the 'tax man'   79

Chapter 8 - Worried I might claim something I shouldn't   93

Chapter 9 - Budgets and savings feel restricting   103

Chapter 10 - I feel icky about having lots of money   110

Chapter 11 - Dislike paying tax   118

Chapter 12 - Not pricing effectively   127

Chapter 13 - Frequently Asked Questions   134

Chapter 14 - A parting gift   138

Contact me   141

Further Useful Resources   143

Acknowledgements   145

About the Author   147

Introduction

According to a popular bookseller's UK website, at time of writing there are over:

◊ 50,000 books on money

◊ 50,000 books on tax

◊ 20,000 books on budgeting, and

◊ 4,000 books on procrastination.

You may have purchased some of these, maybe even read a few and made some small changes, but within a couple of months you likely felt you were right back to where you started. The reason being, in my opinion, is most of these books lack two things, and the good news is this book covers them both!

The Magical Mix of Money & Tax will explore the two important factors preventing you from managing your money and business accounts. It will also assist you with the procrastination you have over doing your tax return by giving you the practical skills and know-how to deal with all the challenges you face, followed by the techniques to overcome them. Essentially this book gives you 12 solutions to overcome these two obstacles across many of their disguises, taking you on the journey from not doing your accounts on time to getting them done on time, being super-organised and happy!

Number one reason why it's not happening yet
Just like learning how to drive, learning how to do your accounts, or manage your money wisely is something we only learn through practical experience and being guided by others.

Having your own business doesn't mean you know what to do when it comes to accounts, finance, tax, budgeting and pricing, but it is giving you valuable practical experience. You may need guidance because no-one has taught you how to do your tax return or manage your money. You've simply been observing the behaviours of others and translating the odd throw-away comment.

Until someone taught you to drive a car skilfully, you couldn't drive - the years you were driven about by others showed you how to fill the car with petrol or what side of the road to drive on, but it didn't tell you the practicalities of how to use the clutch and what pressure to apply on the brake. The same principle applies to your finances.

Over the coming chapters, I'm going to give you **12 guides** that will teach you the basic underlying facts about business finances and managing money. These will walk you through the steps needed to do your tax return easily without stress. These guides will contain **solutions** enabling you to organise your accounts and consist of practical tips and psychological insights.

Second reason why it's not happening yet

It's not happening because you are procrastinating, or sabotaging it, for a reason. The chances are you don't consciously know what that reason is, but this book will help you find out what is holding you back and what to do about it.

You can overcome your procrastination, or self-sabotage, either by changing your behaviour or by understanding your behaviour. Both can work, but the latter is more permanent. When we are consciously aware of what is happening and why, we are more aware of the obstacles that challenge us, which then gives us the awareness to do something about them. Think of it like treating either the cause or the symptom.

Treating the symptom (changing the behaviour) helps you now, but unless you identify the cause (the emotional reason you are procrastinating) the symptom (behaviour) will just come back. We'll explore this briefly across Chapters 1 and 2 and then delve further as we progress throughout the book.

What you will get from reading this book

The Magical Mix of Money & Tax will provide you with the understanding and practical aspects of how to do your accounts and keep them up to date, so you can file your tax return early. It will also show you how to maintain a budget, spend in relation to your business and financial goals, and price your products or services. By the end of this book, you will be closer to your financial success, enlightened about money (and possibly a few other things) and doing your tax return long before it's due - plus hope-fully telling lots of people about how great this book is too!

Warning!

This book has the potential to have you organised with your accounts, filing your tax return, or submitting all the information required to your accountant (possibly saving you money too), within a few short weeks of the financial year-end date. You can file as early as 6th April if you are a UK taxpayer, and depending on the complexity of your business, this is possible (a previous client of mine has filed on the 6th April for two years in a row now) but we'll aim to have you filing by the 30th May each year.

Following the guides in this book gives you the potential to be in a position of knowing your sales and purchase totals easily, either from memory or accessing your accounting software (or your spreadsheets). Furthermore, you'll be pricing your services and/or products more effec-tively whilst managing your time better.

You'll also be budgeting effectively and spending your money more on the things you want and less on the things you don't want. In short, you'll be taking one step closer every day to being in control of your financial success. But you do have to put the work in.

How do I know it works?

I have worked with many business owners over the last 20 years, addressing all of their challenges and implementing all of the solutions. Furthermore, I went through a few of the challenges myself.

Structure

This book contains 14 chapters. The first 12 identify the problems preventing business owners from managing their money and keeping their accounts up to date. These chapters look at both the psychological and accounting explanations behind the problems, giving you an understanding and occasionally a case study to see it in action (all names have been changed except mine). You are then given a solution for you to implement.

Some of the solutions will take you outside this book to templates which you can either download from my website and/or use to consult an accountant or finance coach to learn more. The reason for this is that they are either Excel-based and/or they are based on rates that can and do change. Every effort will be taken to keep these up to date but please ensure you check when they were last updated when accessing them and before taking any action.

The remaining chapters contain a Frequently Asked Questions chapter in true Q&A style for you to refer to time and time again until you learn the UK tax basics. Finally, there is a summary that rounds up the key learnings this book teaches, including the parting wisdom from my 91-year-old gran.

OK, so let's get started!

Chapter 1

Overcoming the distractions
Solution: Identify your pain point and commit to change

I totally get the whole "not wanting to do your accounts as there are far more interesting things to do". Whilst I do like doing accounts, I have days when I'd rather be doing something else too, much more fun, but unfortunately, in terms of boring versus exciting, sometimes we just have to do the boring stuff. Some people also have a "not wanting to pay tax" programme going on in their subconscious belief system (or perhaps it's more conscious in today's political environment!) which holds them back from doing their tax return - but we'll cover that in Chapter 11.

Doing your accounts and tax return is just like brushing and flossing your teeth
Honestly, how excited are you about brushing and flossing your teeth? I imagine the response is "not really", yet we do it because we know only too well the consequences

of not doing it. We soon made sure we brushed our teeth properly after we'd had our first ordeal at the dentist!

The consequences of not keeping your accounts up to date is likely something you face frequently - when sitting surrounded by between three and twelve months' worth of receipts, burning the midnight oil and frantically wishing time could go backwards as it ticks dangerously close to "filing o'clock".

Or it's when you suddenly realise your outgoings are more than your income and find yourself having to give up the freedom of working for yourself and go back to employment. Alternatively, it could be when you want a mortgage or a car loan, but because your accounts are not up to date and your accountant's busy, you miss out on that awesome house or cool car.

Being self-employed has many benefits. You get to choose when you work, how many holidays you take, who you work for and the type of work you do, but like most things, it comes with a trade-off. You may no longer answer to an employer, but you do have to answer to HMRC (or your equivalent tax authority if outside the UK).

Let's do something about this together

I want you to be able to spend time with those you love, have fun, and, if you can afford it, get that awesome house or car. But if you want to remain self-employed where you have a complete sense of freedom and for the first time ever in your life, you feel in control of what you do and when - you have to let me (or your accountant) help you.

You've also got to help yourself

Making big changes and/or being mentored is very similar to losing weight or getting healthy. The packaging tells you how much fat and calories are in the food and, if you have one, your personal trainer will give you exercises that best fit your personality and lifestyle - but it's up to you to discipline yourself with the choice of foods you eat and the exercise you do. Every day is a challenge but with the right support, your weight loss goal is achievable, but only if you take steps towards it and keep your pain point in clear sight.

Generally speaking, you are always in control of piling on the pounds, losing weight or keeping your weight at a steady level. You always have a choice over your actions, but it is incredibly challenging when your focus is elsewhere and you are stressed or worried.

Whether you have been successful or not when it comes to weight loss, the secret to making changes in your life, including doing your accounts regularly and/or managing your money, is:

◊ Take small easy steps each day,

◊ Keep your goal (and what you don't want) in clear sight

◊ Reach out to a friend to help you in the challenging stressful moments.

If you let me, I can be that friend.

The first hurdle
The first step is being disciplined to stick to the plan and not get side-tracked. Admittedly that is hard when you really don't feel like doing your accounts, nor have any passion towards the task, especially when there are other more enjoyable things to do that are much more fun.

Thus the first hurdle is the distractions, otherwise known as the bright shiny objects shouting "play with me!" (In relation to weight loss this would be the chocolate or the piece of cake shouting "eat me!"). The solution is being committed to your promise to yourself.

When you started reading this book, you committed to changing how you felt about money and tax so you could have more time and peace in your life. You promised yourself less stress and more joy. This is all possible, others have achieved it – and you'll hear more about them later - but you must want to do this.

Do you really want this change? Do you really want to be organised with your accounts and feel more at ease with money and tax?

Where to start looking for time to do the non-fun things
Before we go any further, I'd like to make one thing clear. Life is meant to be fun, or at least I believe so, thus we want to ensure we get to do all the fun things we want

to do, but we must make a little room for the not-so-fun things or our life will just come crashing down around us.

First: work out how many hours you have available each week (or month) then roughly split that time between doing the fun things and the not-so-fun things that you know you really must do or there will be consequences. This could be 50/50 or perhaps more 75/25. The choice is yours and will largely depend on everything you do and your attitude towards it.

Second: now we need to know what the consequences are - just like we know only too well, the consequences of not brushing and flossing our teeth properly (after we'd had our first ordeal at the dentist). Keep that fear close to your decision-making when easily distracted by fun things.

What do you fear when it comes to your tax return?

I'm not a fan of fear and self-doubt or anxiety, but they do play a very crucial role in our lives. In my experience, fear always shows up when we're doing something that we probably shouldn't be doing (e.g. bright shiny object/distraction), and we usually experience self-doubt or anxiety when we have rushed excitedly ahead and missed an important step in a process. More than likely, the omitted step is simply asking if this is what we truly want, thus questioning if we are being true to ourselves.

If we let them, fear and self-doubt or anxiety can help guide us into taking the right action.

Take a moment to answer the following 3 questions:

◊ What could happen if you didn't do your accounts regularly?

◊ What has happened in the past when you've left things to the last minute and how did that impact your life?

◊ What could happen if you didn't do your tax return at all?

What does your fear or anxiety tell you? Do you dread the loss of freedom you now have over your day, worry that you'll not have enough money to pay your tax bill, or feel anxious about not knowing what your tax bill is until a couple of days before it is due to be paid?

If you have no fears or anxieties but feel that your inner child is throwing a tantrum because you have to do a tax return (and pay tax!), then I'd like to remind you of something we often forget when we run our own business.

The responsibilities of self-employment over employment
When you walked away from employment, you didn't clear yourself of all adult responsibilities. You simply chucked away the one that said, "I must be nice to my colleagues and report to a boss" and replaced it with, "I have a duty to my clients and the tax authorities".

Furthermore, when you were employed you were paid through the PAYE system (in the UK). You didn't have to concern yourself with the tax due because your employer's payroll system deducted it before paying you. If you paid close attention to your payslip, you may have grumbled over how much was deducted, but otherwise you likely barely noticed it.

Now you're self-employed, you have to manage all that yourself. If that scares you, if that is where your fear lies, then please get the help of an accountant. Shop around for one that you feel at ease with, but do get one as they can help assist you with your tax return and let you know what you can and cannot claim as deductible expenses (see Chapter 8 for more on this).

You can choose to run a business and have greater freedom over your life, or admit the responsibilities are just too much and go back to employment.
Being your own boss, doing the tax return, the accounts and getting the clients is not easy. No-one said it would be, but it can be an opportunity to do exciting things. Yet so can employment. There is no right or wrong. Some of my clients and acquaintances have gone back to employment for a multitude of reasons, primarily because it fitted in with what they really wanted. I almost did too until I re-evaluated my beliefs and aligned them with a business that I wanted and a life which brought me joy.

However, business owners need employees, thus for there to be a balance, some people need to be employees. You may just need to seek out a decent employer (they do exist!) or reassess your client base and self-employed team (those who support you either physically or mentally and emotionally).

The choice is yours. No-one is judging you – least of all me. Your happiness is at stake. Life truly is far too short but we must acknowledge the responsibilities we have chosen to bear, or change course if we can. You deserve to be happy and carefree. We all do.

The next step, if you're coming with me, is to believe that you can find a way to make this work, which brings me nicely to beliefs.

Chapter 2

I'm useless at doing my accounts
Solution: Apply a little curiosity to your cognitive dissonance

You may have heard the phrase *"Whether you think you can or think you can't – you're right"'* by Henry Ford. Or maybe Louise Hay's *"Change Your Thoughts, Change Your Life"*. The concept has got a bit fluffy over the years in my opinion, but the underlying message is the same – if you think you can't do something, you will likely always believe that.

Cognitive dissonance of accounts

If, on the off-chance, something you thought couldn't happen to you, did ever happen you likely thought it was a fluke and sought out a rational explanation for why it happened. There is a psychological term used to describe this called *cognitive dissonance* - it is the process your brain undertakes when it seeks an explanation for the anomalies between your beliefs and your reality.

For example, perhaps something really good happened to you one day and you wanted to know what influenced it so you could repeat the experience (because we always like to be in control!) Maybe your favourite sports team won a competition, or since this is a business book, maybe you won a great contract or signed up a fabulous new customer. If you believed these things didn't normally happen to you, you would have looked for a reason to explain it in order to understand why it happened. You likely then assigned the good luck to whatever reason you came up with.

If we apply this often subconscious psychological brain process to your finances, it's possible that when you have managed your money well and had the savings for your tax bill, and you have been organised with your accounts, you categorised it as a miracle. Maybe the gods were looking down on you, but I also suspect that it happened because you are capable of such achievements when you put your mind to it. It's just that sometimes there is so much other stuff going on.

In short, if you believe that you can't manage your money, keep your accounts up to date and do your tax return, then you will always believe that. But if you were to erase that belief and replace it with "I can manage my money, keep my accounts up to date, and do my tax return", how does that make you feel?

Confirmation bias of accounts

To add to the mix, there is another psychological term which explains why the cognitive dissonance is so strong. It's called *confirmation bias* which is another psychological process that often occurs when we believe something.

Confirmation bias is when we actively look for evidence that supports a belief we strongly hold and, consciously or unconsciously, we adapt our behaviour, where possible, to ensure that what happens next meets our expectation. This is a very common concept in experiments, which is why scientists detail their research workings so it can be replicated by others. No-one is exempt from confirmation bias (nor from cognitive dissonance).

If you strongly believe you can't manage your money, keep your accounts up to date or do you tax return months before the deadline, any action you do take towards this is likely to be sabotaged to ensure your expectations support your belief. This happens so your reality meets your expectation.

An example could be that you get your accounts all organised, but then accidently delete the file a few weeks later, erasing all your hard work. Another could be that you save the money for what you suspect you will need for your tax bill, but a few weeks before paying it, you spend excessively. Admittedly, it doesn't help having Christmas so close to the UK tax payment deadline... Joking aside though, this is why it's crucial you know what your bill is and have it safely put aside before Christmas or even before the summer holidays.

There are moments in life when something happens to which we shout, "I knew that would happen!" This, in theory, is our confirmation bias in action, if the result is something within our control. Effectively, we unconsciously influence the result, so we remain in a world where things happen in alignment with our expectations. Yet a world where we are, at times, pleasantly surprised is available to us if we question our beliefs and become mindful over all actions we take.

Thus when re-scheduling time to do your accounts because something happened that disrupted your plans, or having to find the money for the tax bill as you spent what you'd previously saved, be curious as to what actually did happen and question with compassion, how you may have influenced that outcome.

Furthermore, during times when you have abstained from spending and saved instead, or been strict with your time and done your accounts by saying no to an invitation or request. Instead of attributing a reason why it was a fluke (cognitive dissonance at play), I suggest you start looking for evidence to support why it was possible, and challenge any beliefs that disagree.

Get curious about your beliefs by answering the following 3 questions:

◊ What general expectations do you have of yourself?

◊ What expectations do you have of yourself when it comes to managing money or doing your tax return?

◊ What would be a better reality?

What do you gain by continually thinking you can't do this?

I want you to start believing "I can do this" and start looking for all the signs that tell you that you can (to confirm the belief). Experiment and see what happens. Be a scientist, do it with full awareness of what you could be believing and expecting, or disbelieving and wanting to disprove. Assess the evidence objectively and ask for a second opinion or two!

   I know one of the challenges of doing your accounts or managing your money is not knowing the practical steps to take. This is why I go through these throughout the book, but before we do, you must believe that you can do this.

It is possible and I'll tell you why

Let me tell you a story. I met a lady on a training course, whom we will call Jackie (for confidentiality purposes), long before either of us had a business. Jackie was terrified at the thought of having to do her tax return and this fear was stopping her from having a business, but she was deeply unhappy at her work and wasn't sleeping. She was such a kind-hearted soul who was passionate about alternative therapies, but her job was literally sucking the life out of her. When I realised this, I promised her I would help her each year with her tax return if she started her business.

We both upheld our promise and over the first couple of years, she gained more and more confidence. I was delighted, yet not surprised, when she called me the third year to say smugly that she had done it all by herself this year and didn't need me. She is also in love with her life now and her business is doing great.

Yeeha!

If Jackie, who was once terrified of doing her tax return so much that it was actually preventing her from having a business, was able to overcome her terror and do it herself, then you can do it too!

The rest of this book will give you the practical steps you need to know, along with tips and guidance on changing behaviours and mindset. I will tell you everything I taught Jackie, and soon you too will see just how easy it actually is.

I believe you are an intelligent individual who is more capable than you think, and whilst you may need a calculator, software or a spreadsheet to help you, you can add up and budget your money. These are the basics needed to do a tax return, in addition to knowing exactly what expenses you can claim, along with understanding the tax system itself, but we'll cover those in Chapters 7, 8 and 11.

Occasionally, I hear people say they are awful with money and figures but when I challenge that belief by asking them a simple maths question, they always answer correctly. This reminds them they are not useless - they can do the basics – but they just might need a little help to build upwards from there.

Let's have a go

If you have £10,000 in sales, then bought goods and services costing £4,000, how much is your profit, that you will you be taxed on?

It's not a trick question; the correct answer is £6,000.

Getting back to basics

Maybe you need a little hand-holding to answer the more complex tax return questions. If so, I will tell you where you can get more information easily. If you still wish to give your accounts paperwork to your accountant, (and in some complex cases it's best), this book will at least teach you more about what they are doing which will enable you to understand some of the things they say to you. It may even help you to save on their bill and who wouldn't want that?!

You may also wish to devise a system to keep your accounts organised and up to date, thus you will want to know how and where to start (see Chapter 6), or maybe you just need a little dose of confirmation bias that tells you can do this. In which case, let's get started.

Oh, so you need help with finding the time. No problem, I have already thought of that one. Please continue.

Chapter 3

Where do I find the time?
Solution: Find time in the places you'd least expect it

You run a business which means you're the kind of person who is actively working in your business (generating income) and on your business (planning, marketing your products and promoting your services), plus you're always on the look-out for opportunities. Why on earth would you do something like your accounts regularly and tax return early? After all, it doesn't pay...

Actually, it does. If you've read any of my other books, you'll know I refer to your accounts as your "finance friend". Let me explain: your friends tell you what they've been up to; they share their celebrations and the challenges they're facing, and sometimes may ask for help. Your accounts are the same, they tell you what's been happening in your business, what challenges and successes you have experienced and what your business needs help with.

The only difference is your accounts are not a tangible person and the actions (and non-action) they are telling you about are all yours. Which, to be fair, is why we don't often look at our accounts, because no-one likes exposing our bad habits, weaknesses or faults, even to ourselves! However, do you remember your pain point and your responsibilities from Chapter 1?

What your finance friend can tell you

Your accounts can tell you which actions are giving you sales and which are not. They can tell you which customers, services or products are more profitable and which are loss-making. They can tell you where you need to invest your time, energy and money and where to stop investing your time, energy and money. They can also tell you what you're spending your money on and whether this is giving you an appropriate return or not.

Unfortunately, whilst most business owners do want to know this information deep down, they sabotage their success by ignoring their accounts (but we'll cover that challenge in later chapters). Hopefully, you can see how your accounts can and do pay - they reward you with information on your business. They can be much better than any mentor too, but similar to working with a coach or therapist, you must want to change (which we'll cover in Chapter 5).

Back to time

Ok, now you understand you need to make time for your accounts more regularly but how? You already have a million things to do!

The first step is acknowledging that you can only do so much at any given moment and you only have a finite amount of time – 24 hours a day to be precise. However, assuming you sleep for an average of eight hours, wash daily, cook and eat three meals a day, do a little exercise, and allow a few hours to relax at the end of the day, it only leaves you with a maximum of ten hours a day to do everything else. Not much huh?

Multitasking here we come!

Given the above realisation that you don't have 24 hours a day, **you only have 10 hours**; it's likely you'll be thinking seriously about multi-tasking. But before you do, please know that psychology studies strongly suggest that some forms of multi-tasking are ineffective and, in some instances, leave us blind to crucial information.

For example, research has demonstrated our cognitive abilities (our thinking and physical responses) decrease when we attempt to make a phone call or even just have a conversation with a passenger whilst driving, and we are less reactive to changes in our environment: our field of vision significantly decreases and we fail to see potential hazards in front of us. Whether you're driving your car or working on your business, you must always be watching out for potential hazards in front you!

However, research has also indicated some lighter cognitive multi-tasking can be done well. It is considered the lighter the cognitive load (the requirement to focus and act quickly if needed); the more effective we can be at doing a second task simultaneously. It therefore depends on how much you have to think about and process, thus whether you are accessing the same resources in your brain to do all the tasks required of it.

For example, whilst it's unlikely you can write an email to one person whilst having a completely different conversation on the phone to another, you can talk with your partner about a business challenge whilst loading the dishwasher. In short, you can likely do your accounts in front of the TV, but not whilst driving…

The real answer lies in prioritising

In order to get things done, and done well, you need to schedule your tasks appropriately throughout the week or month. This requires prioritising (which I'll expand on in the next chapter), which to work effectively, requires you to be honest about what you feel you need to do and what you actually need to do. Don't worry about this at the moment; I'll walk you through this shortly.

Once you've done that, you need to compare this with what you can do, and how long each task takes.

Furthermore, it is suggested you delegate the stuff you can't do (whether technically or physically). However, whilst delegating can be a time saver, it's crucial to know it's unlikely you can completely forget about it. It's more likely you can trust that it will get done, but it may still require a little attention from you to check a few things. For example, you can outsource your book-keeping and give your accounts to your accountant to do for you, but you will still need to check that the information they are processing and filing on your behalf is correct.

Let's get started!
To prioritise effectively, I suggest answering the following five questions every time you plan ahead, whether that be your day, week or month.

◊ What is the one big goal/intention for me, my family, friends and business?

◊ What do I want to have happen?

◊ What needs to happen?

◊ What do I want to avoid at all costs? (I.e. your pain point from Chapter 1).

◊ What doesn't need to happen?

It's important to ALWAYS approach your to-do list with these five questions in mind, especially if your time is restricted. I often write my next day's to-do list at the end of the working day (based loosely on the above) then come into the office the next morning asking: "What one thing MUST happen today?" I then do that and if I have time left before heading home, I ask the same question again, and write the following day's to-do list.

You will find the answers bring clarity about what you really need to do. Be mindful of any feelings that come up as you ask yourself these questions as they can sometimes bring up annoyance or frustration, especially Question 5 (What doesn't need to happen?) Answer them based on how you are feeling each time.

Be aware of any resistance that comes too. Like fear, resistance can be useful knowledge! It lets you know that you feel strongly about something so it's important you honour those feelings and listen to them. If however, it makes you feel uncomfortable, then please seek out a coach, a mindfulness teacher or a really good friend who can help you with this.

Are you working to someone else's schedule?
Have you ever considered the possibility of not having enough time because you feel you ought to work within someone schedule? This could be your partner's schedule or your children's schooling.

For example, your partner may be employed, thus even although you're self-employed, you feel you have to work within his/her hours. Alternatively, you may feel you have to work around your children's schooling. In theory, both of these make logical sense and you could do everything you have to do whilst your partner is at work, or the kids are in school, but how is this working for you?

Does this give you enough time to do everything? If not, go back to your answer for Question 1 of the prioritising questions: What is the one big goal/intention for me, my family, friends and business? Is your answer to be available to your family or your clients or both? If you have a business, it's likely that your answer is both.

Be honest about how you feel and what you want

It is quite possible you will feel strongly about whether your family or your business should come first. Please take a moment to acknowledge which it is in this moment. Equally, be aware this can change in the future, depending on what is going on at home or in your business.

For example, your family may come first if your children are young or you have elderly parents. But it could be your business if your partner is out of work, or you're working on an intensive project, or you have a big expenditure coming up and money is an issue right now.

Doing this small, but powerful exercise requires you to be honest about how much time you really want to be spending with your family and in your business. It's also crucial you consider where your friends sit amongst these priorities, and how much time you feel you need for them. Furthermore, ensure you put yourself first occasionally too!

Be very clear about who and what is important in your life. Every decision from here will be much easier once you gain clarity over where you really want to be spending your time.

Time is incredibly precious. We may be able to make more money, but we only have a finite amount of time. Let that fact sink in before moving on.

Perhaps you are working to a previous schedule?

If it's not your partner's job or children's schooling that determines your working hours, you may feel you ought to work around an old way of thinking which no longer suits you. For example, most business owners, when they leave employment to set up their business, end up working the same hours they did whilst employed, but they soon find these hours exhaust them. Gradually, they find their preferred time for working becomes evening or early morning once they experiment with what works best for them.

You likely set up your business for more flexibility around your personal life or to work the hours that suit you the best (depending if you're a night owl or an early riser) - so do it! Experiment until something feels like it fits well.

Getting the structure right

It's crucial, if you struggle to make time for anything, to acknowledge how much time you actually have, in the week or month in question. Then divide up the time between your business (which is further split between client work, sales and marketing, business development, admin and accounts), your close family, partner and/or kids, your friends, extended family and your own nourishment and/or hobbies.

It may seem like too much detail but this is intended only as a guide. For example, when you were at school, you had your timetable for subjects which let you know when you were doing what and when you had to bring your gym clothes or fake an illness...

Joking aside, you're an adult now and you get to choose what you do and don't do. You always have the option to delegate or simply not do something. However, if money is tight, then that's a good reason itself to give regular attention to your accounts. Or if you always feel overwhelmed with everything that you have to do, then getting yourself a structure can be incredibly helpful.

Admittedly, structure like this can often be perceived as being rigid, and yet we do have structure and routine every day of our lives. We have a time when we like to wake up and go to sleep each day, a time we like to eat breakfast, lunch and dinner, and a time we like to start winding down from our busy day. These routines or structures all help our brain to engage with the more demanding tasks in our life by helping it conserve energy from the everyday tasks we routinely do. On a more practical level, it also helps us to plan our days better.

Limit the decision-making where possible
Most inspiring business owners and political leaders in the world, past and present, have other people plan their

diary, and decide what they wear and eat so it's one less thing to think about. All they have to do is show up and do what they do best. For example, it was reported that Steve Jobs wore only blue jeans and a black T-shirt so he didn't have to think about what to wear each day, thus didn't waste valuable decision-making energy over his clothing. How often do you stare into your wardrobe and wonder what to wear today for meeting that special client?

Regardless of what you think of the decisions leaders make, most of them prioritise their cognitive processing for important tasks like running their business or running their country. Perhaps they still make mistakes but just imagine how much worse it could be if they are challenged with what to wear in the morning when meeting an important figurehead, leaving their brain drained of energy for the big decisions.

Findings of the studies into driving whilst talking to someone else, as mentioned earlier, clearly suggest that your cognitive abilities are limited, no matter how good you think you are at multitasking, so take inspiration from Steve Jobs or others. Limit the everyday decisions. You may have access to fewer resources than the top leaders, and less support staff, but you can work with what you have available. Acknowledge the true time you have available, limit the decisions you need to make and ensure you are always looking out for hazards!

Avoid over-promising more time than you can give

Many times, I have tried to give others more time than I have available and sadly, have let my friends down or not got back to my clients in the timespan that I had said I would. Furthermore, occasionally I have found myself unnecessarily stressed when attempting to squeeze in my own accounts after having over-promised more of my time to people and projects than I can give. Many business owners face this same predicament.

It is crucial to acknowledge our priorities, preferably each month, and be clear how much time we have available for our family, friends, business and hobbies. For example, finalising this book was a high priority for me, in addition to managing a busy workload, so knowing how much time I had available to see my friends and business acquaintances helped me to limit appointments or say "no" to non-essential meetings. However, knowing I needed time for myself to rest after a busy week, despite my desire to finish this book, meant there was more than one occasion when I had to move the publishing date. Referring back to priorities, I moved what I could and worked on what needed to happen for my business and own wellbeing, both of which are high priorities for me.

Being disciplined with the time allocated to a task

Saying "no", or being firm with our time, is something most business owners struggle with during the early years of their business. But once they experience their pain point, (that moment I described in Chapter 1 where we suffer badly or lose out on something because we're not organised), they are then more determined to get on top of things.

For example, I've met many business owners who, when cooking dinner for their families, try to reply to emails and text messages or even return business calls. Very often, this resulted in double-booking clients, or not giving themselves time to get from one meeting to the next, thus looking unprofessional or quoting a wrong price! I personally have not experienced any of those, but I have burnt dinner a few times when checking my phone, so now it gets switched off when I arrive home or left at the office.

A little planning exercise

I want you to plan a week based on everything I have discussed until now. It can sometimes be more helpful to look at a month or three months, but when going into this amount of detail for the first time, I would advise you keep it to a shorter timespan until you get used to doing it.

Consider how much time you actually have for everything that is important to you. I suggested it was only 70 hours a week (10 hours a day) at the beginning of this chapter, but if you sleep less than eight hours, or cook meals from raw ingredients then it may it different.

Then, first as a percentage, determine how much time you want to dedicate to your business, family, friends and yourself. For example, if you decided over the course of a week it was 20% family, 10% friends, 50% business and 20% for you, this would result in, (based on 70 hours a week), 14 hours per week for family, 7 hours for friends, and 35 hours for all business requirements, leaving 14 hours for your own hobbies and nourishment.

To get an idea of this on any given day (assuming you work evenly across seven days a week), this would be two hours per day for family, one hour for friends, five hours for business and two hours for your own hobbies and nourishment!

Now it's your turn. What percentage do you want to give to your family, friends, business and time for you? Remember each of the individual percentages must add up to 100. Then you must multiply each percentage by the total number of hours available. However, if you need help to calculate the percentages, you can access a simple spreadsheet from the downloadable Book Resources on my website (see page 141 for details on how to access this).

Is it any wonder we feel we never have enough time?

It's not surprising we feel overwhelmed when thinking about how much time we have available. When we look at the amount of time we could devote to the things we want to do, as well as the things we need to do to run a business – no wonder we feel we never have enough time!

So how do you do it all?

You can't - at least not all in the same day, as we can clearly see. Very few of us would spend 1 hour, including travel time, with a friend over coffee. Perhaps social media platforms are so popular nowadays because most of us are trying to cram so much into a day in isolation, giving the allocated time to our friends each day via online tools.

However, over the course of a week (or a month) you can do it all by making firm choices, getting clear on your priorities, keeping a reminder close to you of what you will suffer or lose if you stray from those priorities. Check in with your intentions and the time allocated throughout each day or week to ensure something hasn't distracted you.

For example, I check in with my planner before I commit to any events or meetings during the working week. However, sometimes I forget, and sadly every time I do, my schedule unravels fast and I quickly feel stressed, overwhelmed and left with a sense that everything is out of control.

I soon learnt I need checks in place to remind me of what I know, however it's also helpful to be aware that whilst planners serve to keep us on track, too much scheduling can feel suffocating. In my experience, it's about balance and knowing what we want and how we need to achieve it.

Experiment with what you feel you need. You could get yourself a coach or mentor to help you with this, but in my opinion, if you can master the act of self-discipline whilst being courageous enough to experiment and reflect on what happens, you will learn skills for life!

Have faith that when you get it right, life generally flows better. You'll make decisions more easily, say "no" to things you don't have time for, or don't want to do, and you'll say "yes" to the things you want more of. Above all, you'll find yourself feeling organised and in control of the things you can directly influence.

Give yourself a proper day off

That said, everyone needs a day off from all business responsibilities once in a while to re-energise, and invite in creativeness, so I encourage you to give yourself permission to have one to two days off from this once a week, or at least once a fortnight, and just go with the flow. However, weird as it sounds, I would suggest you factor this "day off" into your weekly planner, and ensure you do leave that day clear in the diary or it will never happen.

For example, where possible, I keep one day a week free from all appointments, even friends. I do my best to ensure I don't have to be anywhere at any given time. I don't always feel productive but I do get lots of joy being creative whilst writing, baking or paper crafting, or at times resting while reading a good book. Whilst not of all that will contribute to my business (nor friends or family) directly, it does contribute to my joy of life which in turn affects my relationships and energises me. It gives me motivation to keep to the schedule the rest of the week too, because if I don't, I may have to give up this day off and I really don't want that to happen...

Over to you

I want you to promise me (and yourself) you will attempt this, assuming you want to feel less stressed and get everything that you can influence done. Give yourself space to assess your needs and priorities, then check in with this daily, or at least several times a week, yet always being mindful and compassionate when it needs to change.

Another spreadsheet in the Book Resources (see page 141) lists all the tasks we may find ourselves wanting to have happen in our business and shows an allocation of that time on any given day, week, month, quarter or year. You will see quite easily, when you input the number of hours available and what percentage you want to give to things, you rarely can start and complete most tasks in a day, and for some bigger jobs, even a week may be too little. It's quite sobering but incredibly valuable.

When considering your tasks, remember to check in with what you would like to have happen with all these demands on your time (business, family, friends and your own nourishment). If you're not sure how to identify your priorities across these groups (because everything seems like a priority!) then you'll love the next chapter – how to actually prioritise.

Chapter 4

Everything is a priority!
Solution: Always remember your fear and be honest about what you REALLY want

I love helping others with their finances, I truly do, and I would do it every day if I could, but over time, I have come to realise there are other things in my life that matter a lot to me and if I neglect these, life is no longer fun for me.

We can change our beliefs and perceptions around our challenges, but we are limited as to how much time we have available on any given day because we really do only have 24 hours a day which, as stated in the previous chapter, is further reduced to 10 hours after sleeping, cooking, eating and basic self-care are given consideration.

10 hours! If that hasn't sunk in yet, please give it time to do so now
To do what we want to achieve within 10 hours requires us to be focused, firm and disciplined. You can just go with the flow all the time if you want to, but you may

find you don't get where you want to be, and that's ok. Being disciplined with your time might not get you there either, because well... life has a habit of throwing a few curveballs. But being disciplined means it's likely your success rate will be higher than if you were to follow all the bright shiny distractions. However, that depends on what success really means for you.

In my previous book Successful Business Minds, I encouraged the reader to take a moment to define what they really wanted out of life and align it with their business goals. For example, if you want to live a very creative life, you can do that by going with the flow but if you want to achieve or contribute something specific, being disciplined with your time is the only way - at least it is as far as I'm aware. All business leaders, coaches, and spiritual gurus will tell you, you need to take action, and all actions must be aligned with your overall intentions.

It doesn't mean you have to work on your business 24/7 though. In Successful Business Minds, I introduced the concept of making all decisions in alignment across what your heart, soul, mind and body all need and want, therefore it's important that you take this into account when prioritising. I recommend you get yourself a copy of the book if you need help addressing all your needs and wants without deeply-held traditional beliefs influencing you. However, for the purposes of this book, I'm going to assume you already know exactly what you really want.

Let's prioritise!

I believe there is no one-size-fits-all, but I encourage you to take on board some of my suggestions and see if they help. As discussed in the previous chapter, you need to allocate the time you have available across your business, your family and friends (assuming you want to see them!) and anything or anyone else that you wish to give attention to. This includes doing something for yourself that nourishes you and keeps you sane! The latter is incredibly important.

I encourage you to experiment, be mindful that your priorities can, and do, change, and each time you sit down to plan, you need to be clear what and who matters to you. Furthermore, you must be very clear about the consequences of not doing certain tasks.

Example of prioritising whilst mindful of consequences

Reading, learning, being outdoors and doing something creative are what matter to me. My clients, my partner, my close family and friends are those who matter to me. I wish to avoid unnecessary stress that being disorganised brings, including anxiety that comes from running out of time or being late. I also have a need to manage my money.

If I were to attempt prioritising across all that matters to me, I would either run out of money and time quite quickly or be in turmoil whilst those things that matter to me conflicted with one another. Therefore, I plan my allocation of time a month in advance using the method I introduced in Chapter 3. For example, when a friend calls up to ask me for lunch, I know what to say based on the following three-part process:

1. Time with my friend matters to me, so my instinctive response is to say "yes". My monthly schedule allocated time for friends, however, that allocation of time is already used up by other friends so I find myself in a dilemma. I really want to see her so I then look at the pain point I wish to avoid and assess if I can see her without creating any pain.

2. If I don't have enough money to cover an extra lunch this month, I would have to say "no" and arrange another time when I do have money. If I could afford the lunch, or we could arrange something less costly, like coffee only, I would then look at the time I had available.

3. As I'd already allocated all my "time for friends" this month, I would have to take time from another task by asking myself: in what area of my life do I feel in control and ahead of schedule? If there was none then I would have to decline lunch, or coffee, and arrange in a month that I had more time available.

What's your decision-making tool?

The above may seem lacking in love for my friend. Please be assured I love my friends, but over the years I have become more honest about what matters to me. My friends love me too and if they knew that seeing them would cause me to get into debt or be stressed about a deadline, they would be horrified. True friends will support you and your priorities, but you do need to make a little space for them.

Perhaps when you read that you were horrified. You might be different, you may place time with your friends as a higher priority and that's ok. It's your choice. I, on the other hand, like to manage my money well and be organised with my time. This is why our individual personal consequences or avoidances matter when it comes to planning and deci-sion-making. Thus, if what you wish to avoid is upsetting your friends because you declined lunch with them, then go for lunch. If however, what you wish to avoid is not having enough money to pay your bills or being in the dark when it comes to your tax return, then I would suggest you decline the occasional lunch or anything else that you may previously have prioritised over your accounts. Experiment and see what sits comfortably with you.

Prioritising means we have to make compromises

When you spend all your money on one thing, you no longer have that money available for anything else, unless you find more. The good news is we can usually earn more money. Unfortunately, time is not quite so easy to come by.

When you give your time to something or someone else after you've allocated it to one thing, you must acknowledge that chunk of time has now been spent and in order for you to replenish the time taken away from the task it was first allocated to, you must now magically find more time.

Now over to you.
◊ Who is important to you?
◊ What is important to you?
◊ What do wish to avoid?
◊ How much time do you have available?

Important tip!

I would suggest you prioritise yourself first. If you're not nourished and energised, quite frankly, you're no use to anyone. And if you're anything like me, when you don't prioritise yourself first, you'll be bad-tempered, anxious, stressed and likely consuming lots of unhealthy food and drink.

Further questions to help you out
◊ What do you need in order to be on top form?
◊ How much time do you wish to spend with your partner/ best-friend?
◊ How much time do you need to spend with your children (if applicable), separate from your partner or extended family?

◊ How much time do you need to spend with your siblings, parents, aunts, uncles, or cousins?

◊ How much time do you need to catch up on your personal finances?

◊ How long does it take to do the grocery shopping?

◊ How long is needed for visiting the dentist/doctor/ hairdresser?

◊ How long is needed for housework?

◊ How much time do you need for your friends, whether catching up on social media, telephone, text message, Skype or over coffee and a cake?

◊ How long do you need to attend to your clients' needs?

◊ How long do you need for training so you keep up to date with changes in your industry?

◊ How long do you need for your admin, such as emails, phone calls and general paperwork?

◊ How long do you need to get your accounts up to date and be prepared for your tax return?

◊ How long do you need for marketing and/or business development?

Implement and review

Now you are clear on what tasks and responsibilities need your time. All that is left is to take action and implement. Be gentle with yourself at the first attempt and know that you may need to tweak the time allocated to certain things regularly, depending on your needs. After a couple of weeks, allocate some time to review by asking yourself the following questions:

◊ Is this working as you wanted it to?

◊ What needs to be tweaked?

◊ What challenges are you encountering on this?

You may get it wrong. Be ok with that as it's likely it felt right when you planned it, but things changed, as they inevitably do. Life is guaranteed to occasionally throw you the odd curveballs, in addition to your own needs and desires changing as you grow older and wiser!

If it's not working, I encourage you to be realistic about how badly you want your life to be different and whether you really do want to be more organised. No-one can motivate you unless it's what you really want. Perhaps you feel something is far more important than being organised with your accounts. It's ok to admit that but you do have to accept the consequences of it too.

However, if you really do want to be organised and time-efficient (with the occasional day off) I suggest you consider the following areas.

Are you prioritising your accounts?

If we go back to the question in Chapter 1, are you caring enough about your finances to give your accounts priority? Most business owners usually only prioritise their accounts when their tax return is a few weeks away from the filing date. I see this time and time again.

Sharon first came to me in a panic in January (the UK's last month for filing). She was stressed and worried about what to do. Once I calmed her down, we submitted her return and she was overjoyed. She had things under control now and thankfully only had a small tax bill. She was pleased also to hear, due to her financial circumstances, she would get a tax refund the following year, so Sharon booked time with me in advance for mid-April, (the UK's first available month for filing) so we could file the next year's tax return to get her refund as early as possible.

We discussed the steps she would need to take (much like what you'll see in this book) in order to keep up to date and continue doing her tax return in April each year.

However, the following year, new projects had distracted her. She knew she would have to pay tax again but kept putting it off, despite knowing that she could file her tax return early but hold off paying until January. She continued to procrastinate and again left it to January before filing. This time though, although she thought she had enough money to pay her tax bill, she got caught out with payments on account (I'll explain those in Chapter 7) and was left stressed and incredibly anxious that she didn't have enough money to pay her tax bill. She now keeps up to date with her accounts, files her tax return every May and pays HMRC in July and January now that she can budget effectively. We'll cover all this in Chapters 7 and 9.

Sharon's story is not rare and this tells me two things: that most business owners will make their accounts a priority when they know they will be rewarded for doing so; however they procrastinate when they have to pay tax. I'll be going into this in more depth in Chapters 10 and 11, but perhaps you could start looking at the avoidance of your own pain point as a reward!

Are you prioritising yourself?

Do you allocate time in the diary but move it when someone asks for your time? If you do this, then I encourage you to be clear about who and what is important and when. For example, your children may be important when they get home from school and your partner once the kids are in bed. Your clients are important when you're in work mode, but when you're in accounts mode; it's you who is important.

Your finances are an extension of you

Putting ourselves first can mean saying "No" to your partner, children, friends, parents, and clients. Call it what you want but it's setting aside a bit of time for you, which can be hard for some business owners. This tends to apply more to women, due to the social constructs we have adopted, but men can experience it too. It's considered selfish to set aside time out of our working day or week for just us, even if that is just our accounts! Yet it's the most important thing we can do for others.

You must allocate time for you, for the sake of your finances, but it helps if you can associate your accounts with someone who is important to you - your partner, children or parents. For example, how would it feel if you could contribute to the household expenditure and ease the burden on your partner? Or how would it feel if you could take your kids to Disneyland every year? Or how would it feel if your child was ill long-term and your partner could take time off work to look after them?

I recently spoke with a business owner who shared with me that after his daughter was diagnosed with Myalgia Encephalomyelitis (M.E.) his wife left her job to look after her. A year later he was happy that he was still able to support them both but only through being mindful of his accounts.

I too have been fortunate enough to be in a position financially to be able to encourage my partner - after being made redundant – to explore what he really wanted to do without the pressure of just getting the first job available to him. Nine months later he is doing something he always wanted to do.

Both of these scenarios are possible without looking at your accounts if money is in abundance and you never need to concern yourself with it. However, most business owners don't experience this...

Focus and discipline yourself

When self-employed, you are accountable for your time, what you do with it, and when you do it. That is fun at the beginning until you realise that you must engage a little discipline or some tasks will never get done. For some business owners, their passion is motivational enough for them, but as for all the other tasks they have to do, they often lack the oomph to get them started and/or finished.

I realised that the words I used were important to my energy. For example, the phrase "to do" was useful for me to know what I needed to do, but it wasn't motivational enough. After experimenting a little, I came up with phrases like Want-to-do and Must-do, which felt more engaging but they still lacked a motivational edge. I then came up with more fun ones such as Move it Monday, Tango Tuesday, Tick-it-off Thursday, Finance Friday, and Soulful Sunday. Please feel free to borrow these if they resonate, or better still, come up with your own!

Are you really focused on what you're doing?

Furthermore, it can be useful to understand that there is a psychological term called 'attention residue' which suggests whatever you do, the first 30 minutes or so is spent on thinking about the last task you did. This is why you can often get insights and solutions to problems when you're doing something else. However, it can interfere with your ability to focus on the task you ought to be doing now.

I gave loads of time management tips in Successful Business Minds, but one crucial tip I advised was when we need to focus we must switch off emails, phones and most definitely, social media. This might seem a bit alarming to you if you're the kind of person that likes to know what everyone else is doing, or be available to your family, friends or clients at a moment's notice, however if this means you're not getting certain tasks done, then something needs to change.

Whilst you may need to be available in some instances, especially if your children are at school, you can still turn off the emails and social media alerts. You could also perhaps silence the mobile phone too, and then ask those who really need to get in touch with you to use your business landline number instead. You may still need to tell your family they can only call that number during the day, (or whatever time you work), and only in an emergency. Your personal mobile is for your personal time. This will take courage, I know that. This is why being clear about what really matters to you is important.

Are you being honest / effective with your time?

Perhaps you're not being honest about the time needed in certain activities, or maybe you're not engaging in energising and motivational activities. Let's take few examples.

Example I: Watching TV or reading

How many hours are you actually spending in front of the TV? Could this be reduced? Maybe all that is required is honesty about how much time you like to spend watching TV, and thus adjust your time budget accordingly.

Are you reading at the best time for you and are you reading the best choice of books? I love reading and will find any moment to read, but I have noticed that certain books will motivate me, whereas others can make me quite lazy. For example, if I read fiction in the evening, it helps me to unwind but if I read fiction in the morning or at lunchtime, I want to keep reading after my allocated time is up - and often do! Alternatively, if I read a non-fiction book in the morning or at lunchtime instead, it energises and inspires me to get on with my day. However, reading non-fiction in the evening doesn't help me relax as my mind just keeps thinking about stuff!

Example 2: Time with partner/child/siblings/parents...

Is the time with your partner quality time or is it always rushed or are you doing something else whilst you're with them? The more quality time I spend with those I care about, the less time we need to spend together. By quality I mean really listening to them and being totally present with them, not doing it half-heartedly while texting someone else or thinking about work. Could you reduce quantity but increase quality?

Furthermore, do they understand that you have a business to run in addition to everything else you do? My partner, family and close friends know I have a business to run, and how much I enjoy studying and writing books, so they give me the space I need but soon let me know if I haven't seen them for a while!

Example 3: Social media

Are you constantly engaging in social media, always checking to see if your post has been liked by someone, or a friend or client has made a comment?

I shamefully admit I did this a lot, and have since learned it's a psychological phenomenon which the organisations behind the platforms are well aware of! I have since reduced the number of platforms I actively engage with. I can still get addicted easily but I now know I have to discipline myself with it. If I have the app on my phone, I ensure I log out after giving myself a dedicated 30 minutes to engage with the platform, and I always log out from my laptop. I have even gone to the lengths of uninstalling the app from my phone at times.

I soon learned by logging out completely (and uninstalling in the more severe situations), that I felt more grounded and focused. I also noticed I had more time to meet with close friends (which I prefer) and keep on top of my accounts and admin.

Example 4: Housework

There will always be housework and gardening to do so it's hopeless trying to keep on top of it. What will be easier is doing the part of it that annoys you the most if it doesn't get done.

If the kitchen is messy when I walk into it first thing in the morning, it can really set me off on a grumpy and ungrounded day, but I find if I make attempts to clean up as I go, then there seems to be less of it, like washing the dishes before bed or putting them in the dishwasher immediately after dinner before I sit down to relax. However, I know having children can make that task far more challenging!

Have you ever considered hiring a cleaner? Some of my clients swear the cost is more than worth it! Unfortunately, it's not allowable as a business expense (more of that in Chapter 8) but it could free you up to earn more income, thus increase your profits (after tax) to pay for it.

Example 5: Clients vs Friends

I love my clients but they don't comfort me when I'm feeling down or upset, (my partner, mum or close friends do), and if I spend more time on my client work, it impacts the quality of my personal relationships. Equally, the more time I spend with my partner or family and friends, the less time I can spend on my business - which in turn impacts my ability to pay the bills and afford a holiday.

The solution is finding a balance, and if money is an issue, ensuring your price reflects the time you have available (which we'll cover in Chapter 12).

Often, applying all of the above means being someone different. That can require a little boldness on our part, which leads us nicely into Chapter 5.

Now we've established our priorities, let's get down to business – where to start!

Chapter 5

Everyone else does theirs last minute
Solution: Stop following the herd

When it comes to doing your tax return on time and not letting it worry you, this is where being different sits.

Whilst writing this book, I had an interesting conversation with a new business owner. Jenny told me that she'd heard within the business community that a tax return was scary and that it's natural for everyone to avoid doing it until the last month. The former is a myth; the latter is what happens when you follow the herd.

Thankfully, Jenny found herself listening to these comments with a curious mind, questioning whether it was the only option or if there was another way. She attempted putting off doing her accounts and the tax return, but it brought anxiety and stress into her life and it felt incredibly unnatural!

After discussing how she was feeling with a friend she trusted, Jenny was told that it's easy to file your own return, especially after getting some help from an approachable accountant. Jenny got my name from her friend and called me up for an appointment and noticed her stress had disappeared by the time she came off the phone. She still felt a little anxiety but once we had got together and filed her tax return in the summer, she felt so relieved. Her kids had noticed her growing anxiety too and remarked that she hadn't been fun lately, and were not looking forward to the summer holidays, but now that she was happier they were relieved as well!

There are many myths in the business community, just as there are many myths about psychology in the personal development community (you'd be blown away by all the myths out there!) but, like Jenny, I suggest you pause for a moment and ask, "Is there another way?"

I always look for another way too, because I often used to feel that although I'm doing what you're supposed to do when running a business, I would get disappointed that I wasn't achieving what I wanted to, nor at times, was I as organised as I wanted to be. I wrote about my original research in Successful Business Minds but the summarised content is simply: be clear on what you want and be courageous enough to ask for it and dispel all the unhelpful beliefs that stop this from happening.

There is always another way. It's called Your Way
At the time of writing, there are over seven billion people on this planet, which is a lot of people! Whilst it's reported

that we share 99.5% of the same DNA, in addition to having similar genes and traits as one another and our ancestors, there is something very different about each and every one of us.

Scientific research and experiments take representative samples of the population and attempt to apply the results to everyone, but it's impossible. We can gain a general idea as to why something happens or how it happens, but we cannot get inside someone's head. And neither can you.

When you look to others for inspiration, it's essential that you acknowledge that what you see may just be happening externally. You have no idea what thoughts they have or what belief system they are operating. Others may tell you what inspires them and makes them do what they do, but they also have unconscious beliefs that they are unaware of - including me!

With that in mind, it's important that you run your business, do your finances and enjoy your life with your own desires and intuition running the ship, rather than always following the advice of others.

If we refer back to Chapter 1, you can choose whether you care or not. Being different is essentially where I feel the "not giving a f**k" movement excels. You can choose whether you care enough to make time for your finances, to respect them and learn how to do your tax return, or not.

I have no idea whether this is the right way for you personally. I just know it makes me feel better when I do it for myself, and I see it brings clarity and peace to other business owners. However, you might be different and that's ok.

I'm going to share a little secret
Some people file late, don't worry about money and yet they still seem to just breeze through life. It happens. Maybe some people in your network are these types of people. I'm certainly not. The question is, are you that type of person, or are you different?

Perhaps you aren't one of those types but you'd like to be. That's ok. I do too! But any time I don't keep an eye on my finances, I can easily spend money that I really ought to have kept for my tax or another sensible expenditure instead. Therefore, whilst I set the intention to worry less about money, I do make the time to keep an eye on my expenditure, calculate my tax regularly and set aside savings, which all effectively help me to worry less about money and the tax bill.

What would you do differently if you could stop worrying about what others do and their perception of you?

What do you want?
- ◊ Do you want a better relationship with your finances and/or with your accountant?

- ◊ Do you want to file your tax return early, or at least get the relevant information across to your accountant in a reasonable timescale?

◊ Do you want to have a better handle on your money?

◊ Do you want to earn more money?

◊ Do you want to spend less money?

Filing your tax return on time, keeping your accounts up to date, budgeting, spending money only on what you and your family really need, and saving for your tax bill will harm no-one. It's the opposite that can do the harm, bringing with it the worry and stress. In fact, your family will thank you for it (as did Jenny's) as you will be more at peace, not stressed nor worried about a surprise tax bill.

You might even find yourself feeling a little smug for filing your tax return before the summer. I think that's a good thing, and you can proudly declare such. Telling others will not be bragging, it will be inspiring.

The truth

The truth is, everyone wants to file early and be on top of their accounts, or at least that's what everyone tells me. But at the heart of what prevents this from happening is the desire to conform. We all want to fit in, and no-one wants to be seen as the smart ass or the "teacher's pet". While we all want the same thing (to be up to date with our accounting), very few are brave enough to stand out and be different.

Weird as this may sound, for some people this is actually a big thing.

You have the option of empathising and saying, "I filed mine months ago with the help of my accountant," slipping them the details of this book as you head off to have afternoon tea with your friends. Or you can join the herd saying, "This is horrible isn't it, why do we have to do this?!"

I was once teased for being the teacher's pet when I was studying for my accounting qualifications. Like everyone else, I was working full time and found it challenging to fit in homework each week. I did it because I really wanted to gain my qualification, but when I started to get called the "teacher's pet" (by 22-year-olds!) I stopped doing my homework. I soon noticed they no longer teased me, and found myself joining in with their complaints about doing homework whilst working full time. It felt good, I was fitting in - until it came to exam time. I suddenly found myself more stressed than I'd ever felt and for the first time ever, having to cram so much into such a short space of time. I hated every minute of it, and it wasn't much fun for my family either!

Conformity is another psychological phenomenon but there is no hard and fast rule as to why it happens. It's also reassuring to know it doesn't always occur. Research has shown us that we conform approximately only 75% of the time, which means 25% of the time we don't (and that's just from a sample of people). I personally think it has to do with whether we're being mindful of our actions and curious about the reasons for doing so.

Speaking from personal experience, I was in a new city with no friends so I really wanted to make friends as well as getting my professional qualification. Once I realised I was valuing making friends over my qualification, I went back to doing my own thing. I then started to attract friends who were more like me: friends who valued their profession, their career growth and did their homework.

Do what's right for you

Everyone is entitled to do what they want in their life, as long as no-one gets harmed in the process. However, if another person's behaviours are holding you back from being organised, managing your money, saving for your tax bill, earning more money and making a profit, then you need to know that you are free to choose to do something different.

If we refer back to Chapter 2, most people don't think they can be organised or have the skills to do their own tax return. In fact many people – just like some of the people Jenny was listening to - think it's the norm to do your tax return at the last minute. I'm here to tell you it's a myth I don't engage with and after over 20 years of working in the accountancy profession, it's actually wearing a bit thin. Furthermore, it brings so much stress to business owners and their accountants.

It can be done and now we've laid the foundations, the next chapter will give you the how.

Chapter 6

Not knowing where to start
Solution: Knowing where to start

Often, once a business owner has acknowledged the benefits of keeping their accounts up to date and filing their tax return early, in addition to any psychological blocks that may be holding them back, the next stumbling block is simply the practical steps on what to do, and more importantly where to start.

Like achieving any goal, the concept of breaking it down into small manageable chunks applies with your accounts and tax return too. You may be up to date and looking for ways to stay up to date or you may have a backlog of at least twelve months to wade through, so I'll approach this from the latter position.

Got mountains of paperwork to wade through?
If this is you, then let's start at the beginning with small steps, and I am going to assume that you have a separate bank

account for your business. Furthermore, when I refer to cash purchases, I'm talking about purchases that are either paid by cash and/or purchases you pay for personally that don't go through your business bank account. However, if you use your personal account a lot, you'll have to add your personal bank statement to the steps I discuss below.

It is always advisable that you separate out your business and personal banking, paying for all business expenses through your business account, or you'll just keeping giving yourself extra work when it comes to doing your accounts and tax return. Therefore it's highly recommended that you set up a separate account for your business immediately. If your business is a limited company, then it's deemed a legal entity in its own right and it MUST have its own bank account because in essence it's not your money until you take it out as salary or dividends.

Part I

Gather together all your expenditure receipts for the period that you are covering.

Count how many months you are covering in this period and get some large envelopes to cover the number of months e.g. April to March is 12 months so get 12 envelopes. If it's now January and you have last year's tax return to do as well as getting the current one up to date, that will require 21 envelopes, in addition to a lot of time and patience...

Label these envelopes with each month so one is called April, another May and so on. Be sure to write the year on them too. This comes in handy if you are covering more than 12 months, or looking for a receipt at a later date.

The UK tax year is officially 6th April to the 5th April the following year, so you have three options:

1. For the April envelope, have a smaller envelope within it that holds just the 1st to 5th April receipts so you know where to find these.

2. Label each large envelope 6th to 5th (e.g. 6th April to 5th May, 6th May to 5th June).

3. You can choose to tell HMRC your financial year is 1st April to 31st March, and work with each month. Note, if you have received dividends or are received any other income (except self-employed earnings) you must include up to 5th April on your self-assessment.

Allocate yourself some 30-60 minutes in your diary each evening (or another convenient time) to spend going through your expenditure receipts and allocating them to the relevant monthly envelope. For example, something bought on 10th May 2018 goes into the envelope labelled May 2018. This can be done in front of the TV or listening to music or doing any other low cognitive task.

At this point, disregard any concerns as to whether or not you can claim a particular expense unless it's obvious you can't e.g. clothes for the kids, as this will only slow you down. We'll cover what you can and cannot claim in Chapter 8.

Part 2

Once you have all the receipts in envelopes, then you need to move on to Part 2. I have made a few suggestions on how to do this, but everyone is different so feel free to come up with your own system, knowing that the intention of Part 2 is simply to check that you have all the receipts.

You may feel you don't need to concern yourself with this task if your sales were low and you know that you have no tax to pay. (Currently there is a £1,000 annual revenue threshold where you don't need to give HMRC your expenses). However, you'll need to get organised with all this when you do start earning more money and need to pay tax, so why not start today? You're delaying the problem if you don't.

Furthermore, if you have made a loss, you may be able to offset this against other income in the year, carry forward to a future year, or carry back to a previous year and get some tax back.

You may also want to tackle this task all in one sitting, so give yourself a few hours.

Follow this method if you like spending time on your pc/laptop/tablet and you're ok with spreadsheets.

Download your bank statements as a csv file (which can be easily saved as an Excel sheet).

Add up all your sales and make a note of the sum, separate from your purchases. If you have made any cash sales, then ensure you add the value to this figure.

Take the relevant month's receipts from your envelopes, and match up to the purchases entries on your bank statements.

Type in, next to the bank statement entry, what it is you have bought (a brief summary is sufficient).

Make a mark on the receipt to indicate you have matched it up, in case you get disturbed whilst doing this.

Repeat until you have gone through all your paper receipts. If you have found cash (or personally paid) receipts, then add these to your spreadsheet but make it clear these are cash, not bank transactions (i.e. paid outside your business bank account).

If you have entries on your bank statements that you have no receipts for, you'll then need to search through your emails (or online accounts) for any PayPal, eBay, Apple, Amazon or credit card purchases. This is to ensure that you claim every-thing you bought and that you have receipts for everything, which you will need to show if asked by the tax authorities.

Follow this method if you prefer to spend very little time on your pc/laptop/tablet.

Print off your bank statements (if you don't already have paper copies).

Manually add up all your sales and make a note of the sum. If you have made any cash sales, then ensure you add the value to this figure.

Take the relevant month's receipts from your envelopes and match up to the purchase entries on your bank statements.

Write next to the bank statement entry what it is you have bought (a brief summary is sufficient).

Make a mark on the receipt to indicate you have matched it up, in case you get disturbed whilst doing this.

Repeat until you have gone through all your paper receipts. If you have found cash receipts (i.e. personally paid), then put these aside until you are finished.

Once finished, list all your cash purchases either on a spreadsheet or on a piece of lined paper and attach all the cash receipts to the back of it, either for each month, or for the year all together.

If you have entries on your bank statements that you have no receipts for, you'll then need to go onto your computer and search through your emails and online accounts for any PayPal, eBay, Apple, Amazon or credit card purchases. This is to ensure that you claim everything you bought and that you have receipts for everything if asked by the tax authorities.

Follow this method if you love being at your computer and you have an online accounting software programme such as QuickBooks, Xero, FreeAgent or Sage.

It is likely you have already imported your bank statements, in which case you just have to reconcile. This is exactly what the two options above were doing, but you're doing it directly with the help of the software so it speeds things up for you. As you identify each item, you categorise it within the software automatically, which saves you doing part 3.

As per above, highlight on each receipt that you have matched this off, and keep cash receipts (i.e. paid for personally) separate. You can then add these to the software as expense claims. Remember to add on any cash sales too.

Going forward, it's good to upload copies of the business receipts to the accounting software which can be done easily if it's an electronic receipt, (sent to you by email). Otherwise, the app version for your phone, or a compatible receipt app, will allow you to take a photo of the paper receipt and upload it to the software.

Part 3

Part 3 is when we categorise the transactions. Currently, this is not essential for your tax return if your sales are below £77k but it is a useful process (which you will find out in Chapter 8) and it helps you become more mindful of how much you are spending on certain items such as travel, refreshments or training.

For those who have accounting software, this is all done for you and can be found in the P&L reporting section. For those who are using spreadsheets, you can either do a data sort then add up each category, or you can do a simple pivot tablet. For those who are doing it by hand, then it's time to get your calculator out, look back to your bank statements and cash report, then add up all the travel, then all the stationery, all the postage, etc.

Over to you now

What more can I say other than pause, put a bookmark in this book or click on a bookmark if reading it online, and get to it!

You may want to read on if you feel you want more information around the tax return before doing this, or if you want to know what you can claim (but this may slow you down in Part 1 of the process) or perhaps you are stalling for a few other reasons (which I'll cover in Chapters 8-12). If, however you are procrastinating for the reasons we have already covered in Chapters 1-5, then please acknowledge stalling only leaves you with less time to do the stuff you need to do. Please re-read!

Perhaps you really don't want to do this and would rather delegate your accounts to a book-keeper, which is perfectly ok. At least this chapter has given you an insight into why your book-keeper's bill is high and helped you to value their work.

Now we've pulled all the book-keeping together, you need to grasp an understanding of the tax return itself, which we cover in the next Chapter. Then in Chapter 8, we'll cover what you can claim.

Chapter 7

Fear of the 'tax man'

Solution: Understand the tax return basics

If you don't know how to do something and/or fear making a mistake, then of course you're going to procrastinate on it. It's natural you're going to hold back from doing anything too grand if you are not sure how the tax system works and what you can claim, or how to fill in your tax return. This attitude is actually very common. It's why most UK accountants are in demand over the winter months when everyone in their first year of business starts to panic and doesn't know what to do.

But it stops now.

I will tell you what to do, what you can claim and where you can go to find out more information. You may still need to seek out the wisdom of HMRC or an accountant for more specific questions, but this chapter will cover the basics.

Over the years I have noticed that a lack of knowledge around the facts about Income Tax (and Corporation Tax) stops many people from filing their tax return (or giving their accounts to their accountant) on time. They don't understand why they are paying a lot of tax some years and very little in other years.. Or worse, why they end up paying too much tax! This is why I think it's important to address the facts around tax here.

Understanding the tax basics – Income Tax

You still need to know about Income Tax rules if you are a limited company, for dividends and other income purposes.

The UK tax year runs from 6th April to 5th April so at the time of writing, we were in the tax year 2019/2020 (6th April 2019 to 5th April 2020). The filing date for online returns is 31st January each year, as is the final payment. Most business owners have grasped this. However, the following facts are less widely known until you experience them.

HMRC 'payments on account'

For those with little profit or low taxable earnings, you will only ever experience payments due on 31st January for the tax year ending on 5th April, the previous year. However, when your profits increase (thus tax due increases), you will find yourself paying HMRC the tax due on 31st January and 50% towards the current tax year you are in, plus a further 50% by 31st July.

These 50% requests are known as payments on account. The 31st January payment on account is a contribution to the current tax year you are in, and the 31st July payment is a further contribution to that tax year. This effectively means that if you were to do your tax return the following January, you would have already paid the tax due for that year, assuming the business did the same financially as the year before. Remember, you will have to continue paying 50% payments on account but by this time it will just be the next tax year rather than the previous tax year too!

This change takes place when the tax due goes above £1,000. This can come as a shock to most business owners, which is why I always recommend doing your tax return early so you know about stuff like this as soon as possible and can start saving, if you haven't already got something put aside.

This can be better explained by an example

For the tax year 2015/16, Susan's tax due for the year was £500 and she was asked to pay this by 31st January 2017.

For the tax year 2016/17, Susan's business profit increased and her tax due for the year was £1,250. However, when she submitted her tax return, she was asked to pay £1,875 by 31st January 2018 (and a further £625 by 31st July 2018). The £1,875 due on 31st January 2018 was made up of the £1,250 due for the 2016/17 tax year past, and £625 (50% of £1,250) towards the current tax year (2017/18). The £625 due on 31st July is the second 50% payment on account towards the 2017/18 tax year.

For the tax year 2017/18, Susan's business profits increased a little more and her tax due for the year was £1,400. When she submitted her tax return, she was asked to pay £850 by 31st January 2019 and a further £700 by 31st July 2019. The £850 due on 31st January 2019 is made up of the £1,400 due for the 2017/18 tax year, less the payments on account made already for 2017/18 (2 x £625 = £1,250) plus £700 (50% of £1,400) towards the current tax year (2018/19). The £700 due on 31st July is the second 50% payment on account towards the 2018/19 tax year too.

A note of warning – online scams

HMRC will never email you with information about your tax code or about payments overdue on your account. There are lots of junk emails pretending to come from HMRC. Please ignore them and delete. HMRC will only ever contact you via the post or via your online account. They may email you about webinars or other similar information, but like your bank, they will NEVER ask you to log in to your account via a link sent by email or similar.

Not knowing how to fill in the return itself

The online return is quite easy to complete and at the time of writing, the interface has recently been upgraded and is more pleasant to interact with. There are six important facts very few people know before doing their first return (or even after doing for it a few years) so I'll discuss each one so you can be well-informed.

Fact 1: Knowing what to claim

Many business owners are not entirely sure what to claim. I cover this in more detail in the next chapter, however HMRC has detailed guidance for sole traders (and limited companies) on their website regarding what can and cannot be claimed.

Please do NOT ask other business owners as each business will differ depending on their situation and industry, and remember that a limited company is different to a sole trader. You may not be familiar with what legal entity a business owner runs his/her business as; therefore you could get wrongful advice.

Call up HMRC's helpline if you have any doubts, or better still, phone your accountant as they will know you and your business well enough to give you bespoke advice. If you have any doubts or fear around claiming something, then it's likely not a valid expense, but please check first before either throwing out the receipt, or worse, claiming because a fellow business owner is doing so.

Furthermore, if there is something you're thinking of buying and not sure whether you can claim it, most accountants are happy to answer any queries you may have. In fact, they'd rather you are proactive as it may turn out there is a better solution for you, depending on your business or circumstances, which could save you money.

Fact 2: You can save the return as you go

Each "page" has an average of 6 questions and has the ability to be saved so you can stop at any time if you need to find additional information or just take a break. Furthermore, whenever you hit "next" to move on to the next page, it will automatically save everything you inputted for that page.

Fact 3: Information is available on most questions

HMRC have an explanation next to most questions telling you what is being asked and what kind of things they are looking for. It can be found by clicking your mouse on the little question mark icon next to the question. I have also included a basic step-by-step guide to the tax return in the Book Resources to help you too (see page 141).

Fact 4: No-one sees the form until you hit submit

If you make a mistake by saying "yes" instead of "no" to a question, it's ok as you have the opportunity to review the full tax return before submitting. Furthermore, sometimes saying "yes" incorrectly to a question means you will be asked other questions that are not applicable to you. This section can easily be deleted by clicking on the "delete this page" option (if applicable). If you don't see the "delete this page" option, it means that these will just be the general questions everyone has to answer. You can change any information, delete pages, add pages and change data before actually submitting it.

Fact 5: You have full control over when (and what) you submit

You CANNOT accidentally submit the form. When you are ready to submit the return to HMRC, you are asked to confirm it's complete by ticking a box and will also be prompted to input your user ID and password again. Thus there is no way that you can accidently hit "submit" in error. This does mean, however, that if you have drafted the return and gone away to check something, you must remember to go back in and submit before 31st January. If you have the return sitting there in a draft format but not submitted, HMRC will see that as an unfiled return and charge you penalties and interest.

Fact 6: A return can be amended if accidental errors or omissions come to light after submission

If you thought everything was all fine, submitted the return and then noticed there was an error, you have the ability to amend the return before the filing date. In fact, currently you can make adjustments up to 31st January the following year. This would only apply if, when doing the return the following year, you realise something should have been answered "yes" or "no" to, or a sale/expense should have been included in the previous year's return. I would recommend that you do your best to get it right first time though, but know there is a facility if you do notice any accidental errors.

However, deliberate errors or submitting false information on purpose will be treated very seriously.

Knowing how much tax will be due for cash flow/saving purposes

Many business owners put off their tax return because they don't know what their tax bill will be. It is far from a logical approach, but humans are rarely logical or rational, as many psychological studies suggest. We put things off because we fear them, which often make the problems worse, or we make irrational decisions – we choose highly impossible gains over very probable losses.

If you are like this, know that whilst it's not a rational action, it's an unconscious defence mechanism that is trying to protect you. Hopefully by now you have gained a desire to know what your accounts are telling you and be able to avoid your pain points. Thus bring compassion and a desire to understand yourself better whilst you explore the reasons behind your action, inaction and/or fear.

Imagine if, like Susan, you discover you have to find £1,850 on 31st January to pay your tax bill when you were expecting the figure to be similar to the previous year (£500). Imagine if you didn't have the money to pay it, like Sharon in Chapter 4. How stressed would you be? What would this do to your family?

However, imagine if you had filed your return on the 31st May and whilst you still didn't have the money, you had eight months to save the additional £1,350. How much happier would you be about that, once you got over the initial shock?

Which scenario would you rather find yourself in?

To help you, I have included a simple Excel spreadsheet in the Book Resources (see page 141 for the link) which will calculate the tax due based on a simple Income Tax return. I have created two different templates, one for Scotland, (currently on slightly higher tax rates), and another for the rest of the UK.

Cloud accounting software

There is currently software that enables the user to file their personal tax return through Cloud/online accounting software, but it's crucial you check the accuracy. I have assisted business owners who have incorrectly coded an expense within the software which resulted in an inaccurate tax return. In one instance, the business owner would have overpaid the correct tax due, but in other instances, the business owners would have underpaid their tax which would incur penalties and interest. In short, take care when coding up your data.

Understanding the tax basics – Corporation Tax

If your business is a private limited company, you have an additional tax year to understand, over and above the tax year for Income Tax. This is called your Company Financial Year.

Your company year-end will be dependent on the date you registered it with Companies House. You can apply to change this date, but it will always be 12 months, with the exception being the year you shorten or lengthen it and the year you first start trading.

You have two filing dates, one for Companies House and the other for HMRC (at the time of writing) - but most accountants will just focus on the earliest of the two - and you have one payment date for your Corporation Tax. The Companies House filing date is nine months after your financial year-end (there is however an exception to this rule in your first year). HMRC's filing date is 12 months after your financial year-end, but their date for paying Corporation Tax is nine months and one day after your financial year-end, so most accountants will just concentrate on the nine-month Companies House deadline. The extra three months for the Corporation Tax return can be useful, but only in exceptional circumstances. For the purposes of this book, we'll focus on the Companies House filing date.

The above can be better explained by two examples

Example I

Jim registered his business on 10th November 2015. His first year's accounts were 10th November 2015 to 30th November 2016, (almost 13 months). Companies House requested that his accounts were submitted to them by 10th August 2017 (nine months after the initial 12 months) and he was due to pay his Corporation Tax to HMRC on the 11th August 2017 (nine months and one day).

The following year, his accounts covered the period 1st December 2016 to 30th November 2017, (exactly 12 months). Companies House requested that his accounts were submitted to them by 31st August 2018 (nine months after his year-end) and he was due to pay his Corporation Tax to HMRC by 1st September 2018 (nine months and one day).

Subsequent years will remain as a 30th November year-end and 31st August/1st September filing and payment date.

Example 2

Kirsty registered her business on 22nd June 2015 which would mean her financial year-end was 30th June but she requested to change this to 31st March. Her first year's accounts were 22nd June 2015 to 31st March 2016. Companies House requested that her accounts were submitted to them by 31st December 2016 and she was due to pay her Corporation Tax to HMRC on the 1st January 2017.

The following year, her accounts covered the period 1st April 2016 to 31st March 2017. Companies House requested again, that her accounts were submitted to them by 31st December 2017 and she was due to pay her Corporation Tax to HMRC on the 1st January 2018.

Subsequent years will remain as a 31st March year-end and 31st December/1st January filing and payment date.

Filing your limited company accounts

Most limited company businesses get an accountant to help them with their company accounts. The reason for this is because their accounts can be quite complex and limited company accounts and Corporation Tax are quite different from sole trader accounts and Income Tax. For more details on the difference, speak with an accountant or visit HMRC's website.

However, assuming you have a grasp of the accounting concepts, the differences between sole trader and limited company, and your company accounts are fairly simple, at the time of writing HMRC allow you to file your accounts through their website. You must also file your accounts with Companies House, but this can be easily done by logging into your Companies House account and keying in the balance sheet data.

Given the speed of technology, it is possible in the future, that there will be accounting software available to you - not just accountants - that will enable you to submit your limited company accounts online. However, at the time of writing this book, I'm not aware of any, other than HMRC; it's currently a manual input.

Similar to your self-assessment, there are late penalty fees and fines imposed on any late filing by both Companies House and HMRC. Furthermore, deliberate errors or submitting false information on purpose will be treated very seriously.

Knowing what to claim

Like sole traders, many directors of limited companies are not entirely sure what to claim but this is covered in more detail in the next chapter. Equally, you can find guidance for this on the HMRC website. As advised before, do NOT ask other business owners as every business differs to another, depending on their situation and industry.

If you can't find the answers on the HMRC website, try their helpline, or speak to your accountant as they can give you bespoke advice. If you are unsure if you can claim something, then it's likely not a valid expense, but check first before throwing anything away, and importantly, don't claim it just because a fellow business owner is doing so. Most accountants are happy to answer any queries you may have.

Knowing how much tax will be due for cash flow/saving purposes

Many directors of limited companies will put off giving their accounts to their accountant because they don't want to pay their Corporation Tax. This is a non-logical approach as mentioned previously.

You do not have to pay anything to HMRC until the deadline (generally nine months and one day after your year-end). However, if you do pay it before the due date, HMRC applies credit interest to your account which will help with next year's Corporation Tax payment (unfortunately they don't do this with Income Tax). In addition, knowing the tax has been paid - and one less thing for you to worry about - can bring massive relief to most business owners. It frees up headspace and brings peace to their finances.

Corporation Tax is currently 19% for small businesses, which will be reducing to 18% on 1st April 2020. Any assets you buy can be offset against your profit through capital allowances but you must add back in depreciation, entertaining and non-allowable charity donations.

Hopefully by now you have grasped a better concept of the UK Income Tax return and the accounts system for limited companies, which now allows us to move on to what you can claim.

Chapter 8

Worried I might claim something I shouldn't
Solution: Know what is allowable by spending money on the right things

As mentioned in the previous chapter, it's important that you understand what you can and cannot claim. An accountant who understands your business - even if it's someone you only see occasionally – can answer such questions. However, I appreciate that most small business owners feel they can't afford an accountant. In most instances, paying for an accountant can give you peace of mind over your tax return if you have any niggling doubts, and may save you money on your tax bill. Furthermore, you don't have to see them every year either. Some accountants will have clients who only go to them every two or three years when something changes within their business or just as a check-up that everything is ok.

If you don't have an accountant, or you would like to reduce your accountancy fees, a good rule of thumb is to ask: "Would I have made this particular purchase if I hadn't been in business?" If your answer is "Yes, I would have bought it anyway", then it's highly likely it's NOT allowed to be claimed in your business. If your answer is "No", then it's possibly a claimable expense, BUT it still must meet the following criteria:

◊ Has the expenditure contributed to your business?

◊ Have you received any income directly (or indirectly) from this expense?

If your business has benefited from the expense, but so have you personally, then often only a percentage (in proportion to your business/personal use) is allowable.

Let's use the example of your broadband service at home. In this modern age, most homes have broadband, thus the cost of such is not a business expense. If, however, you had to upgrade to a faster download package due to your business needs, then it could be argued the increase in cost (total cost less the price you paid before) is a business expense. If you took advantage of this faster package and used it to download films for personal viewing, then only a portion of it would be allowable, thus you would have to significantly reduce, or eliminate, the business claim in relation to the personal use.

Another example would be the utility costs incurred whilst working from home in your business, thus using more electricity and gas than you would if you were out all day. You can either calculate exactly how much extra you are using, or the preferred option would be to adopt HMRC's simplified flat rate method which you can read about here: *https://www.gov.uk/simpler-income-tax-simplified-expenses/working-from-home*. (Please note, this link was correct at time of printing).

For other common examples, please visit my blogs but do remember to seek professional advice relevant to your industry and circumstances.

◊ *https://www.hmcoaching.co.uk/ what-can-i-claim-as-a-business-expense/*

◊ *https://www.hmcoaching.co.uk/can-i-claim- lunch-dinner-refreshments-in-my-business/*

Furthermore, HMRC have great guidance on their website and they will be happy to answer any questions you have by phone. Remember, do NOT ask other business owners. Every business is different. Get your own accountant or phone HMRC.

Overcome the avoidance of looking at accounts

Often business owners delay meeting their accountant in order to delay the inevitable – the discussion about a lack of profit. They have usually either made a loss or 'broken even' (their sales match expenditure) and are ashamed. Personally, I think this issue is why a lot of business owners dread visiting their accountant or don't employ one.

Many business owners believe their annual meeting will mean their accountant is going to pull them up about their expenditure, in particular they're going to have to face the reality of how much they have spent on something, and they really don't want to know in case they have to cut back on it. Or they feel they will have to face up to the reality of how the business is performing.

Whilst all those things will happen, what the accountant is really doing is:

◊ Analysing the expenditure to help the person get a sense of what costs are crucial to the business. These are called fixed costs and help to accurately calculate the optimum pricing for the business.

◊ Addressing whether the business is operating efficiently or not, and making suggestions.

◊ Assessing the reasons why the business is not performing well financially and help the business owner with the challenges they are having with this.

Not looking at your accounts is simply a form of denial, which is a psychological defence mechanism, but also detrimental to your business. We've all experienced denial and other unconscious defence mechanisms through-out our lives, and will continue to do so, but when they become unhealthy for either you or your business, you must become mindful of them and take action to mitigate them.

Perhaps you are anxious about paying more tax than you can afford, or fear your business will go bankrupt, so you don't look at your accounts, thus avoiding the reality of it. Unfortunately, not looking at something in order to avoid it means you're far more likely to end up experiencing the very thing you are anxious or fearful about!

Not looking at your accounts will lead to a high possibility of unexpectedly having to find the money for a large tax bill. Furthermore, the likelihood of bankruptcy is certainly higher for those who refuse to pay attention to their accounts.

HMRC are unsympathetic when it comes to your unconscious psychological behaviour – in other words, there is no excuse and you will be penalised - but there is a solution to address this.

How you feel about spending money stops you from filing your tax return on time

How you feel about money and why you feel the need to buy things will all play a part in how you feel about looking (or not looking) at your accounts. I discussed this in detail in Successful Business Minds, but I'll give a short overview here.

You may think you are good at managing money but what you don't know is the conditions have to be right for that. Up until now, you have just been lucky with receiving money. For example, Jane had a few regular clients whose work she relied upon to pay her rent and other costs. These were fairly high-profile businesses but within a week, two of her highest-paying clients decided to cease their budget for the work she did for them. She suddenly found herself with no savings to tide her over until she replaced the clients. She was in a very stressful situation. To make matters worse, she had a tax bill coming up which she had planned to pay with the money from her client's next invoice.

Always have savings for the unexpected and put aside money now for tax to pay on these earnings. Tax, or any other costs, should never be paid from future earnings. Your business MUST be able to pay your overheads and tax due on today's profits from today's money. If you are unable to do this, then your business is not being efficient or you are withdrawing too much personally. I highly recommend you look at your costs and how you have calculated your price.

On the other hand, you may think you spend money efficiently but the conditions have to be right for that too. If you are happy, you may have a tight control over your expenditure, but if there is an upset in your private life, you may go on a spending spree. If you find yourself in Jane's situation at the same time, it will only hurt your finances.

Keeping an eye on your accounts can tell you these things, which is why it's important you are mindful and address them head on. Any avoidance such as not doing your monthly accounts nor your annual tax return, will only prolong the pain, the guilt, the receipts piling up, the money going down, the tax return unfiled and the fear of the unknown.

Instead of beating yourself up and avoiding the information, get curious

Track your expenditure and be mindful of any feelings that come up when you do. Do you feel guilt or anger?

Do you keep procrastinating when you know you should sit down to do your book-keeping? For example, do you decide that it would be better for you to go for walk, have a slice of cake, or a glass of wine? There is nothing wrong with any of these actions, but if they happen every time you sit down to your accounts, then they are likely a defence mechanism in place and the longer you ignore what you're avoiding, the more painful this will be, time and time again.

Try to take small steps to become more rational and feel better about spending. By being more assertive over your purchasing, you will be less likely to avoid looking at your accounts.

Calculate the return on investment on all expenditure

When a business buys anything, there are three steps the decision maker should take to assess the return it will give back. If you do this, you can easily take control over your expenditure and it will encourage you to take the emotion out of money, which it is highly charged with.

Most organisations know that when you buy something, your emotions are involved. Even your need to earn money is highly emotional and they use this to their advantage. If you can become less emotional about money (spending and receiving) you begin to take back control. I discussed this in detail in Successful Business Minds but to get a head start, you can do the following 3 steps:

◊ Calculate what financial return the product or service will give you (see below).

◊ Compare the results (again, see below).

◊ Check in with your "four minds" (cognitive, emotional, somatic and intuitive) – see *Successful Business Minds* for more on this or visit *https://www.hmcoaching.co.uk/how-to-make-a-quick-decision.*

Asking "Why am I buying this?" is something that most people avoid, hence why many business owners don't like looking at their finances. However, to assess the potential financial return of something you are buying for your business, you MUST look at the return it ought to give you over a four-year period.

There are three methods that accountants will use to calculate if an investment is worthwhile but for the purposes of this book, I will focus on just one – how quickly you can get your money back.

The length of time you are prepared to wait to get your money back will depend on your financial situation and how patient you are. However, for a simple rule I would apply the following:

◊ Paid back within 3 months: go for it.

◊ 4-12 months: go for it if you have the funds to keep you going.

◊ 1-2 years: proceed if you have a good stable income.

◊ 2-3 years: proceed with caution.

◊ 3-4 years: hmm, it's getting risky. How accurate are your calculations and what conditions are they based on?

◊ 4+ years: it is incredible risky now. I would consider the stability of the return in addition to all of the above recommendations.

Each expenditure will be different, which is why there are other methods to assess the return on an investment. Your own financial situation will influence this decision too. It is also important that you feel motivated to do it, can do it physically and emotionally, and you are addressing your underlying need.

What if you don't think the purchase will give you a return at all?

If you don't think the purchase will give you a return, then I would ask you to consider why you are buying it. If you are buying something for pleasure, and almost impossible to quantify, I would question whether it's a business expenditure at all.

If it is stationery then it will be providing a use, but it is still challenging to quantify a return, therefore, if money is tight, then you need to ensure you are not buying the more high-end brands if they are not going to contribute financially. On the other hand, software and/or a computer that can save you time or reduce outsourcing costs has quantifiable savings which you can easily match it against.

It is important to be mindful of what defence mechanism you are feeding when you buy something. For example, when Linda was looking to purchase and attend another training course, she thought she was learning and adding more skills to the already full toolbox, but she soon realised that she was attempting to buy confidence; something she knew would only come through taking action.

Gemma was similar when she signed up to an expensive coaching programme that promised her a £1m business in less than six months. She was pretty certain the cost would soon repay itself but after paying for it with a credit card, she soon realised all it was telling her to do was take action, which she knew deep down before she signed up. She felt humiliated and ashamed. Sadly she isn't the first to desire change so badly she'll pay for a quick fix. Unfortunately there isn't one.

Nothing will change in your life without action and mindfulness, which brings us nicely to our next chapter: feeling good about budgeting and saving.

Chapter 9

Budgets and savings feel restricting

Solution: Look for reasons to feel good about budgeting and saving, by knowing you're taking care of yourself and taking steps towards your goals

You may think you're ok with managing your money but the moment someone says "budget" or "save", do you suddenly feel restricted? If so, this likely brings out the rebel in you - a bit like eating an extra slice of cake because someone tells you not to, even though you were feeling quite full! Thus, any mention of budgeting and saving likely gets you thinking about buying that new coat you've been eyeing up, or that holiday you've been putting off until you can afford it.

You're an adult - of course you don't like being told what to do! Be assured I am not here to tell you what to do - I hate being told what to do too. However, the fact you're reading this book tells me you're looking for some suggestions, and as a colleague recently remarked, when someone gives you advice, they are usually only doing it because they care.

It matters to me that you fill your tax return on time, that you know how much tax you're going to have to pay, and that you have enough money in the bank to pay it. I care that you're on top of your accounts and feel organised and know what's coming in and going out of your bank account.

Why do I care?

Firstly, on a practical level, I care because I may bump into you in the supermarket queue and perhaps you're grumpy or rude to me because another month has gone by, the filing o'clock deadline is getting dangerously close and you're no further forward. Or maybe I meet you on the roads and you're really stressed because you don't know what your tax bill is going to be, and you hit my car whilst coming out of a junction because you were too preoccupied to see me.

Secondly, I care because seeing clients stressing out about their accounts and wondering how they're going to pay their tax bill creates anxiety for most accountants.

Thirdly, I care because I have a huge passion for preventing poverty and homelessness. I'm not suggesting it will happen to you and your family, but unless you have a huge reliable and steady income which you know for sure is greater than your expenditure, it is always a possibility: a client may suddenly no longer need your services; your partner may get made redundant; a family member may be taken ill and you need to spend time with them.

James, who I met recently at a homelessness conference, shared with me that he had once ended up homeless and on the streets because he split up from his wife and struggled to pay off his debts. Another, Stuart, just had a run of bad luck when it came to jobs and landlords.

Poverty and/or debt can mean many things but at the very lowest level of the spectrum, it means being unable to afford the essentials for you and your family. No-one can predict the future so it's always advisable to have a financial safety net in place for unexpected financial challenges. Jane, who you met in the last chapter, never thought she would struggle financially – her business was going really well – but things soon changed when her two largest clients walked away.

There have been moments in my own life where money has been scarce, and I know in most instances it could have been avoided by taking action sooner and being mindful of expenditure. That said, sometimes life throws a few unexpected challenges that you can do nothing about, which is where having a little spare money helps, even if it's just to treat yourself in order to cheer yourself up!

Why does the absence of budgeting and savings stop you from filing your tax return on time?

Aside from all the other challenges listed in this book, most people hold back from filing their tax return because they haven't held back any savings, or budgeted appropriately for the tax bill and are scared that they'll have a large tax bill to pay. This procrastination is the defence mechanism denial I mentioned in the last chapter.

Budgeting basics

The underlying foundation to budgeting is to balance the money coming in with the money going out, essentially accounting for everything you spend. I covered the problem with spending money in the last chapter, as it holds some of us back from budgeting. Thus, assuming you've become more mindful and rational with your spending now, we'll move on.

Budgeting assesses income (sales, earnings or salaries) and expenditure – effectively balancing what's coming in with what's going out and forecasting in advance the big expenditure like tax bills or holidays.

Budgeting is quite simple in theory, but it can fail when we make too many assumptions which is why we also need to have a 'rainy-day' fund. This requires putting some money aside – over and above the savings for the projected expenditure we do know about - for something we don't anticipate yet, but when it happens, we will be a little prepared. If Jane had budgeted and had a rainy-day fund, she would have had money set aside for the tax bill and equally, some savings to tide her over until she replaced her two big clients. However, she struggled financially for almost a year.

Budgeting in action is taking the following action when

you receive money for your services.

◊ Estimate your Income Tax and put it aside into a savings account (approximately 15% but will depend on your overheads).

◊ Assess what current bills need to be paid and pay them.

◊ Forecast what future expenses you have and put aside some of today's money for that (approximately 10-20%).

◊ Put at least a further 10% aside for a rainy day.

◊ We are then free to spend what we have left. Easy, right?

Unfortunately, most business owners don't go through the actions above, or they are unable to. Some find themselves anxious as they are constantly in financial stress, wishing it would all just go away, yet budgeting and saving can bring such a relief. And then there are those who aren't making a profit so there probably would be no tax to pay, but as they are already in financial difficulties, budgeting is crucial.

In the Book Resources, you will find a spreadsheet that will help you with the above (see page 141 for more details on how to access this).

How do you budget when you don't have the money?
Sadly, there is no overnight magic formula to dispel financial stress. It takes time and effort to tighten up your spending, analyse your expenditure, and look for ways to

save on costs (both in your business and your personal life). It also takes discipline and mindfulness to address your unconscious actions and inactions (i.e. understanding your defence mechanisms).

In times of financial stress, the holidays away from home and other treats or luxuries may have to be postponed to pay your tax bill and get some savings under your belt. HMRC no longer accept personal credit card payments to pay tax due, and whilst they may agree an instalment plan in very rare and exceptional circumstances, you will still be charged penalties and interest.

I once had a high credit card bill and the only way to pay it off was to stop using it and cut it up. I appreciate that cutting it up may not be practical if you feel you need to keep it for emergencies. In this case, I advise you take it out of your purse or wallet and either lock it away in a drawer or give it to someone you trust to keep for you, and be very mindful of everything you want to buy.

Furthermore, get creative with your services and products to increase your sales. I discuss in another book 12 Steps to Improve Your Cashflow how we can often be motivated when cash is tight to do something we had once seen as scary. When we are comfortable, or at least have access to credit, we're less likely to do something challenging. But when we have to find the money from somewhere to pay a bill, it can often be a good thing for our business as we come up with something new and innovative.

Interestingly though, having lots of money in savings can actually be one of our budgeting problems too, which brings us nicely to the next chapter.

Chapter 10

I feel icky about having lots of money
Solution: Feel ok about receiving money

It is quite possible that you are not allowing more money into your life for fear of judgement. That could show up through an ineffective price structure or by spending constantly.

Alternatively, maybe you spend time with people who complain a lot, they are in "victim mode", blaming Brexit and everything else for their current situation. That doesn't mean the situation they find themselves is their own fault, but this outlook can be infectious and we do have a choice as to how we respond to our environment. Businesses can fail in a recession, but businesses can flourish too - just pick up any decent business book to find out how, but I'll save you the bother and the money. It's all to do with attitude.

Everyone is entitled to their belief system, but only at their own expense. If someone else's beliefs are holding you back from being organised, making a profit and having a healthy savings account, then you have a choice as to whether you continue to associate with them or not. However, if these people are your close friends and family, then I would recommend you find a way to allow them to believe what they want but for you to do what is right for you and your business.

I discussed in depth a few of the primary reasons that money could be holding you back in my previous two books. 12 Steps to Improve Your Cashflow covered a few issues such as thinking differently about sales and expenses, and addressed behaviours and mindset. Successful Business Minds then delved deeper into the mindset around money and success. For the purposes of this book, the following section covers one of the important issues I addressed.

Money is a very versatile tool

In its simplest form, money is a tool used to exchange our time to buy property, goods and services required to meet our needs, plus the occasional luxury. Once known in the form of notes and coins, nowadays, with the use of cash declining while the use of cards increases – leaving out the cryptocurrencies for now - it's becoming just a series of numbers you see on your bank statement. Unfortunately, what is also happening, is that we are emotionally connected to what money can buy us and what it means from a status position, i.e. when we have less money than our friends or neighbours. In short, money has become associated with our self-image.

How do you really feel about money?

How you feel about money will originate from something someone told you when you were young, or something you have experienced yourself. Some of the beliefs that are lurking around in your subconscious could be "money is the root of all evil", "money doesn't grow on trees" and "money doesn't make you happy", but they all have something in common. They are myths, or perhaps more aptly defined, they are innuendos.

The following is an exercise I have revised from Successful Business Minds. Please take a moment to answer each question honestly.

Money Exercise

It is recommended that this exercise is done often, at least annually, but more if you are having money problems. Often, we can have more than one belief about money, thus it's likely when you first do this exercise you will work with the most pressing issue you have, but there could be more. I have certainly uncovered more than one when coming back to this exercise at different times in my life.

◊ Pick up some coins, (any denomination will do), close your eyes and jangle them about in your hand. What thoughts, feelings, sounds or images do you hear, feel or see?

◊ Get hold of a £5 note and stare at it for one minute, turning it over in your hand, then put it in your pocket for a moment and bring it back out. What thoughts, feelings, sounds or images do you hear, feel or see?

◊ Repeat the above with a £10 note, a £20 note and a £50 note if you have one (or get one from your bank). If you don't carry cash around with you, look at the pictures I supply in the Book Resources section (see page 141 on how to access this), and imagine they are in front of you, or attempt to visualise them now. What thoughts, feelings, sounds or images do you, feel, hear or see?

◊ Now look at your bank account and notice the balance. What thoughts, feelings, sounds or images do you, feel, hear or see?

◊ Now imagine you have £100,000 in your bank account. What thoughts, feelings, sounds or images do you feel, hear or see?

◊ Now imagine you have £1 million in your bank account. What thoughts, feelings, sounds or images do you feel, hear or see?

Doing the above exercise will enable you to become more mindful of what you think about money and whether you have any unconscious beliefs that could be sabotaging your business finances. For example, Cheryl did this exercise and recalled an experience where her grandfather gave her a £5 note and her brother, a year older, a £10 note. This action had encouraged Cheryl to believe that men can expect more than women which had resulted in her undercutting her pricing which was causing her business to lose money. This was soon rectified once she realised it was just something her grandfather had done and had meant no harm.

When Duncan did this exercise, he found that he when he imagined he had a £1 million pounds, he felt he would have to hide it from his family as he imagined they would ask him for some of it. This was based on a time when he was younger and had savings. His older brothers had borrowed money from him and never repaid it. They felt that since he had plenty he therefore didn't need it. As Duncan felt powerless against his brothers, he imagined he would soon lose the million pounds. When Duncan realised where this deeply-held belief came from, he realised that he was deliberately sabotaging the financial success of his business so he didn't have money to give his brothers. He rectified this by exercising courage in saying "No" to his brothers and seeing that his own financial success was nothing to do with them.

How do you really feel about receiving money?

How you feel about asking for and receiving money will be a factor in how you feel about looking (or not looking) at your accounts. If you have any unhelpful subconscious beliefs about money in your belief system, you will unconsciously be avoiding doing your accounts so you don't have to face them. You're running a business, thus anything that tells you that you're not doing very well will result in your old friend denial coming to visit.

You may think you are ok with asking for money but again, in actual fact, the conditions have to be right for that. If you have old hang-ups about asking for money from friends, family, or strangers, then you may find yourself unable to have proper business discussions, or find yourself offering them a discount because you feel uncomfortable taking the full price from them.

For example, Mark was totally cool with taking money from strangers for his products, but any time his family or friends asked for something, he gave them a huge discount. Naturally, this was not helping his profits. Once he had the courage to speak with them about it, he realised they were embarrassed that they kept getting discounts, and it was actually preventing them from buying more from him!

Another exercise

I want you to imagine that you are walking along a street near your home when a kind stranger approaches you, carrying a bag. They smile at you and say, "Hi, you don't know me, but I know you very well. I would like you to have this gift," and they hand you the bag they are carrying. You open the bag and look inside to see it's full of £5, £10, £20, £50 and £100 notes. As you look up to speak to the stranger, they have mysteriously disappeared.

What are you thinking? What are you feeling?

Now consider the same scenario, but this time that person is a friend and they are still there when you look up.

What are you thinking? What are you feeling?

Now consider the same scenario again, but this time with a family member.

What are you thinking? What are you feeling?

Now I would like you to recall times when you accepted money from your customers.

What are you thinking? What are you feeling?

Do either of the money gift scenarios above match how you feel, or what you think, when your customer pays you? Does it depend on who the customer is?

I hope you took the time to do the exercise above. It can be incredibly powerful in accessing your subconscious beliefs about receiving money. Mark realised he was making his friends and family uncomfortable by giving them a discount which was preventing them from buying from him, in addition to reducing his profit. By doing the above exercise he was able to increase his profits and sell more!

Perhaps there is fear

Could you be deliberating sabotaging money coming into your life for fear of what people will think? If so, I encourage you to read Chapter 5 again. You're also going to love the story about my gran which I share in the closing chapter of this book, but first consider how Duncan realised he had to be more assertive with his brothers. Who do you need to be more assertive with?

Perhaps you don't like the idea of paying tax? More money means more tax, right? Let's move on to Chapter 11.

Chapter 11

Dislike paying tax

Solution: Change your attitude to paying tax

In the current political climate, it's possible you may not want to pay tax to your government, but if you truly want your business to be a proper business (even if it's just you) then there is no easy way to say this. Accept that paying tax is just something you have to do, and the more tax you pay, the more successful your business is, but we'll cover this in more detail throughout the chapter.

The rate of tax you pay will depend on where you live and what you get in return. You have chosen to live in a particular country, use their roads and services and run a business in that country. That, for most countries, involves paying tax. You always have the choice to move to a country where the taxes are lower, if that matters to you.

Some people dislike paying tax because it feels like being punished, (I'll expand on this later), the extra admin burden or simply because they dislike their government's values and/or the way their government is spending their money. It's understandable yet it's holding you back from being organised and achieving the financial success you desire.

What can you do about it?

You can do something about the issues that anger you but you must acknowledge and let go of those things that you can't do anything about. Changing the government minis-ters who make the decisions on behalf of your country is something you can change. Paying tax is the one thing you must accept.

That might sound like a bit of tough love, but other than getting behind a lobbying party to change how the public sector spend your taxes, or ensuring that your business is being tax-efficient, there is really nothing more you can do. In the meantime, accept it for what it is, let go of the grudge and move on.

Truth be told, you're actually self-sabotaging your success by getting hung up on this. I'm not kidding. No, this doesn't mean that you sit back and watch your government destroy everything your ancestors built up, but fight it in a more productive way that doesn't hurt your finances. If you reduce your sales to pay less tax, it only hurts you as you then have to claim benefits to pay your rent, and then you're truly dependent on the government. Is that what you want?

Do you want your government to control every aspect of your life or would you like to be in control of your finances? In this case, you can change your attitude towards tax and see it as a reward. Humour me for a bit and read on.

Another way to think about tax

There are several psychological schools of thought on how to motivate people. Some behaviourists believe reinforcement (negative or positive) works, whereas others believe punishment is more effective (negative or positive).

Reinforcement is when something is either given to you or removed from you to encourage the desired behaviour. **Punishment** is when something is either given to you or removed from you to discourage the undesired behaviour. Positive reinforcement/ punishment occurs when something is given to you, negative reinforcement/ punishment is when something is removed from you.

In the example of keeping up with your accounts and doing your tax return, a positive reinforcement would be that feel-good feeling you get from being organised. A negative reinforcement would be when HMRC stop sending you reminder letters. Alternatively, a positive punishment would be a fine for late filing. A negative punishment would be if you were to lose your business and were declared bankrupt.

If you have your accounts up to date, file your tax return on time, feel good and HMRC are no longer sending you reminder letters, this reinforces the behaviour for you to keep doing this. You still have your business and you're not penalised with a fine, thus you're not being punished, which is a bonus and a good indication you're on the right track!

But a negative punishment is the removal of something and this is where the problem lies with how some business owners see tax.

The current psychological problem with paying tax

Forgetting for a moment the political landscape – if you can - the problem people have with paying tax is that they see it as a punishment for their success.

Every business owner I know is motivated to do their tax return as soon as they can if they are likely to get a tax refund (i.e. they are given something they want – money!) If, on the other hand, they know they will have to pay tax, then they stall because they see it as a punishment. Their money (hard-earned in most cases!) is being take away from them.

For example, Tanya's accounts reported a significant increase in sales from previous years, resulting in an increased profit before tax of £20k. Her tax bill for the limited company was £4k more than the previous year and her personal tax bill was £2k more (due to an increase in dividends taken). Her reply when told the amount of tax due was: "I feel punished for my success."

Tanya has always delayed sending her accounts to her accountant but this year she was quicker off the mark as she wanted to get a mortgage, but it didn't make her feel any better about it. As Tanya neatly summed up, tax is seen as punishment for doing well.

Pete, another business owner, referred to HMRC as the school bully. When his tax bill was confirmed, he replied saying he wasn't going to invite HMRC to his 50th birth-day party...

Very few people want to pay tax, but I challenge Tanya and Pete's attitude, and I encourage others (including you) to view paying tax as a sign of financial success!

Of course, it's important to establish that your expend-iture is tax-efficient and get yourself an accountant if you need help. An accountant will guide you in ensuring your business is being efficient when it comes to tax, but they will not help you to AVOID tax. Tax avoidance is illegal. Furthermore, contrary to what the media report, anyone - no matter how famous - will be prosecuted if they are actively avoiding tax. It is a serious offence.

We live in a world where we have to pay for healthcare, education, sanitation and street lighting, amongst other things. Tax is what pays for this. If you look at your online account, it tells you what your tax is paying for.

For example, the 2017/18 report I received from HMRC told me my tax paid towards the following:

Where it went	Share
Welfare	24%
Health	20%
State Pensions	13%
Education	12%
National Debt	6%
Defence	5%
Public Order & Safety	4%
Transport	4%
Business & Industry	3%
Government Administration	2%
Culture (sports, libraries & museums)	2%
Environment	2%
Housing & Street Lighting	1%
Overseas Aid	1%
Contribution to EU Budget	1%

Some people think the current system isn't effective but until we can come up with an alternative that works, or lobby to change it, we must accept it and pay our taxes. Alternatively, consider for a moment the consequences if everyone decided not to pay tax. Where would your child go to school? How would you get a doctor to treat your elderly parent or your best friend if she gets cancer? Where would you get funding to learn a key concept in your business?

Frustrations with politicians can be detrimental to your business

Most of today's politicians fail to inspire me but I don't let them hold me back. Do you?

There have been lots of 'developments' in the world of politics across the UK, America and Europe lately and whilst I don't feel this is the time or place to discuss these changes (there are other great books out there that do), it is important to address this issue in relation to your business.

I have seen many clients who are annoyed at paying more tax and feel angry about all the money that is wasted across the public sector. Whilst I agree to some extent with how they feel, this attitude can be really bad for business because their sales and profits usually start to take a dip. You need to be mindful that your energy, thoughts and attitude are all influencing your financial situation.

Another event that often causes sales and cash flow to dip for small businesses is when they reach the VAT threshold.

What happens when a small business hits the VAT threshold

Some small businesses (especially sole traders/one-director companies) are very conscious of the VAT threshold and have a fear of hitting that level of sales. They are very conscious of keeping their business small so as to avoid the admin burden of VAT. This was very transparent in one client I had.

The advice that follows applies to the UK only. Other countries have different rules.

Heather's sales were rocketing during the first five years of her business and she was really excited about the future but she was caught off-guard with VAT. Heather had reached the VAT threshold, but had been unaware of it until doing her annual accounts. Together with her accountant, she registered for VAT and continued to charge VAT on her sales, but then her sales dropped so Heather deregistered. Two years on, her sales were continuing to fall. Because she had ended up having to pay what she considered an "extra tax" and had not been prepared for it, it had a detrimental effect on her business finances. Like Tanya, she felt she was being punished for being successful, in addition to feeling ashamed for being disorganised.

The VAT threshold runs on a 12-month rolling system, which means that it's on any cumulative 12-month period, not your annual accounts each year. You must register immediately once your sales for any 12-month period go above the threshold, and charge your customers the sales tax. If you miss it and/or don't charge your customers the sales tax, then you could find yourself with a large tax bill. This is why you will find a few horror stories out there about being VAT registered, but I address these in Chapter 13. Keeping an eye on your accounts ensures you take timely action.

Over the years, I have seen many business owners having to uncover unconscious beliefs about tax and money in general as they reach the VAT threshold. When they reach this infamous milestone, it can bring many unconscious negative money and tax beliefs to the surface. However, if they are addressed quickly, despite a little wobble in sales, most of them continue to do well and rise up to meet the next business challenge!

If you proactively earn money and take steps to change your attitude towards tax, the next thing that could stop you from doing your tax return is your pricing structure. Your accounts reflect the decisions you've made over the previous twelve months, and if your prices are too low you will be reminded of this when it comes to your tax return. However, your defence mechanism kicks in and helps you to avoid facing up to it until the last minute when you don't have time to fully concentrate on it. Yup, our old friend denial again!

Consequently, if your prices are too low, you will find you don't have the time to take out of your business to do your tax return, because you're having to spend every waking moment earning money!

Either way, please move on to the next chapter for the last solution.

Chapter 12

Not pricing effectively
Solution: Price effectively

When you came up with your price, how did you do it? Did you look around and see what everyone else was charging or did you just pluck a figure out of thin air?

If you answered yes to either of the above, I believe this is another subconscious reason why you put off doing your tax return and accounts. Deep down, you know your price may not be quite right and you don't want to be reminded each time you look at your accounts.

You are not alone. Most small businesses do this, however, that is not the right way to calculate your price. In the Book Resources section (see page 141 for more details), I have included a template that will allow you to price your products and services more effectively, but I will give you a summary below.

Charging per the hour

◊ First work out how many hours you can have available for your business. Remember Chapter 4? Put this aside for a moment.

◊ Count up all your business expenditure and your personal expenditure.

◊ Divide your total expenditure (Step 2) by the number of hours you have available for your business (Step 1). Then to calculate an amount to cover things like tax and unexpected expenditure, multiply your answer by 1.5. This gives you an hourly minimum rate. Acknowledge now that if you ever charge less than this, you will be unable to pay your bills.

◊ Take your minimum hourly rate (Step 3) and calculate the following 3 amounts:

◊ Multiply it by another 1.5.

◊ Double it.

◊ Multiply it by 3.

◊ Sit with these four figures (the one from Step 3 and the other 3 from Step 4), then based on your integrity and your customers' affordability, assess which one you wish to charge.

Example of hourly rate pricing

Kate has 15 hours a week available in her business to work directly with clients, but she takes six weeks annual holiday, so during those weeks she is unavailable to work. Her total business expenditure is £500 per month. Her total personal monthly outgoings are £1,500 and her husband is currently employed and contributing to this. However, for the purposes of budgeting for the unexpected, we're going to assume Kate's business has to be able to support both her and her husband's personal finances, or at least find out what she would need if she had to.

◊ Step 1 - We work out how many hours she has available a year: 15 x 46 weeks (52 weeks a year less six weeks for holidays), gives us 690 hours in any given year.

◊ Step 2 - We work out how much her expenditure is a year: £500 a month (business) + £1,500 a month (personal), which gives us £2,000 a month x 12 months, gives us £24,000 a year.

◊ Step 3 – To work out what her hourly rate should be, we divide £24,000 by 690 hours, which gives us £34.78 (to the nearest penny). We then multiply this by 1.5 to cover a few unexpected expenses, which gives us £52.17.

◊ Step 4 – we multiply £52.17 by a further 1.5, and 2 and 3 to get four other figures for Kate to contemplate.

This means Kate is meditating on an hourly rate (to the nearest pound) of £52, £78, £104 or £157 for a price that sits with her ethics and integrity. Depending on Kate's type of customers and the service she offers her clients, she will choose somewhere between £52 p/hr and £157 per/hr. The important thing to remember is that she should NOT go below £52 because if she does, she may find herself unable to pay her bills if anything happens to her husband's job or they find themselves with an unexpected expense to pay.

Hopefully you understand the importance of working out the price that is right for you and ensuring that if anything happens, your business can support you and your family. If not, please re-read the solution to Chapter 10.

Now it's your turn.

◊ Total hours available =

◊ Total business expenditure, plus total personal expenditure =

◊ Annual expenditure divided by annual hours available to work, multiplied by 1.5 =

◊ Taking figures calculated above, multiply by 1.5, 2 and 3 =

What four prices do you have? How do you feel about these? Which one feels right?

What happens if you don't charge by the hour but by project?

Do the above exercise to get the minimum hourly rate and then work out how many hours you likely spend on each project.

What happens if you sell products?

The price is calculated on a similar basis, but you must take into account the individual costs of each product. I have included a basic costing spreadsheet in the Book's Resources (see page 141), but for a complex manufacturing business I would advise you see an accountant.

What happens if your minimum price is more than everyone else's?

It's quite likely other businesses aren't charging enough to cover their costs, or have not done such a detailed calculation as you have. As mentioned at the beginning of this chapter, many business owners have simply picked a price out of a few random numbers that were running around their head.

Furthermore, it's highly likely they are not budgeting for any unexpected events such as their partner being made redundant, or having to leave their job to look after their sick child or elderly parent. Doing so is a personal choice at the end of the day. You don't have to do this either, but it's good to get a grasp of what you would need to suddenly increase your prices to if that did happen to you.

Just imagine how you will feel knowing you don't have to worry about any unexpected expenses.

For example, if Kate hadn't worked out that she need to charge a minimum of £57p/hr to cover personal finances too, she could have been charging a minimum of £13 p/hr, which is significant different!

But what if my customers won't pay that price?

Perhaps your customers will be unhappy with the increased price. You won't know until you try. You must also assess whether they are the right customers for you if you can't afford to pay your bills (unless you look at ways you could reduce your outgoings).

I've met a few business owners who thought their customers wouldn't pay their higher price, only to find out it was ok. They understood and valued the service they received. In these instances, the business owners weren't valuing themselves. An option though, is to keep your old price for your existing customers (although I would advise that you increase it a little if significantly different) and then charge the new price just for new customers.

In Successful Business Minds, I share an example of a client who went through a similar exercise and immediately increased her price. Suzy was totally blown away by the new customers accepting her price without any queries, and she had no bother from any of her current clients when she raised her prices either. Once she discovered her price had been below the minimum she needed to pay her bills, she understood why she had struggled and incurred losses for several years prior to meeting with me. After she increased her price, she felt so relieved knowing she would always be able to pay her business costs and personal bills.

At the end of the day, you can charge what you like - assuming your customers are happy to pay it - but my hope is that the above exercise will get you thinking a bit more about your budget and how you could be better prepared for unexpected expenses. Then you can feel at ease with your finances and maybe feel better about doing your accounts on time, knowing that you're taking charge of your business.

Throughout this book, I have only ever made a suggestion that will help you be more organised and proactive when it comes to doing your accounts and tax return. Implementing any of these are your choice.

You picked up this book to find a way to do your accounts and tax return with more ease and overcome any overwhelm. You may now realise, hopefully several chapters ago, that this book gives you much more than that.

Before we say goodbye, I have one more story to tell that I think you will like. There is also a chapter addressing the frequently asked questions I and many other accountants get asked, along with the book's resources.

Chapter 13

Frequently Asked Questions

Can I claim tax paid as an expense?
No. Income tax is a personal expense that is due on the profits you make. Corporation Tax is a business expense after profits have been calculated.

Can I claim National Insurance paid as an expense?
If you are a sole trader, no. Similar to above, National Insurance tax is a personal expense that is due on the profits you make.

If you are a limited company, only Employer's National Insurance is allowable as a business expense.

Can I claim business assets bought as an expense?
Yes. You must exclude the cost (and depreciation) from the profit calculation and add only the cost under the capital allowances section of the tax return (applies to both Self-Assessment and Corporation Tax). There is a separate section for declaring assets and claiming an investment allowance.

I have heard that business owners lose out once they become VAT registered. Is that true?

No. Business owners only lose out when they become VAT registered because of two reasons:

◊ VAT is, as the name suggests, a value-added tax. It is added onto the sale price but some businesses keep their price the same and don't pass on the tax charge to their customer.

◊ They have failed to keep an eye on their sales and reached the VAT threshold several months ago. As they can't go back and recharge VAT to their customers, they have to pay it themselves. I gave an example of this in Chapter 11.

I have submitted my tax return and my tax due is not showing on my account. Does this mean HMRC have not received my return?

It's unlikely, if when you submitted your return you were given a submission receipt reference (always best to write it down or do a screenshot). Often it can take a few days for it to show up as due on your account. However, if the computer crashed as you were submitting it, it's likely that HMRC didn't receive it, but you will see it still sitting waiting to be sent if you go back into your online account.

HMRC are telling me I owe a fortune. Why is that?

Check to see if they are asking you to make a payment on account (re-read Chapter 7). Furthermore, bear in mind the tax due amount, shown just before you finalise your return, does not include payments you have already made. Wait three to seven days and check again. The amount due will be:

◊ The tax due based on the return submitted
◊ Plus the 50% payment on account for next year (if applicable)
◊ Less the tax already paid on account (on 31st January last year and 31st July just past).

What happens if I cannot submit my accounts/ tax return on time?
You will be charged penalties and interest by HMRC and, if a limited company, Companies House too.

What paperwork do I need to have to submit my tax return? Do I need to keep receipts and invoices?
You must keep bank statements, receipts and invoices for seven years, even if you have Cloud accounting. Also be mindful that if you keep all your receipts online, the software must be backed up. If you use Cloud accounting software, you will either have to stay with that supplier or export all your details before closing your subscription.

Do I have to fill in a tax return if I have a second job/ small business selling things online?
Currently, at the time of writing, if your total sales (that's income, not profit) are under £1,000 you don't need to, but

if you have received dividends over £2,000 then yes, you need to add these to your tax return.

Chapter 14

A parting gift

I hope you enjoyed this book and are now on your way to filing last year's tax return, (if it's still not done), and making great progress with this year too!

Remember to identify your pain point and commit to change, question your beliefs and be very clear about the time you have available and what your priorities are. It's crucial you take action, be mindful of how you feel about money and your attitude towards tax. Furthermore, be very clear on what you can claim and what return your expenditure is giving you. In addition, ensure you're budgeting and pricing effectively. Above all, stop following the herd and ensure your actions contribute to your own personal and financial goals.

Before we say goodbye, I want to share with you a motivational story about a lady who inspired me for over forty years and continues to do so through the stories my family tell.

Flora was a very special lady who endured a lot of challenges in her life and although she grumbled (don't we all?!) she would just get on with whatever hand she was dealt. She lost her husband in a road accident when she was in her thirties, leaving her with three children all under the age of eleven years old. She worried a lot, yet she knew that she could only change what was under her control. Flora was always there for anyone who needed her (family, friends, and especially stray cats...)

During the Second World War, when Flora was of eligible age, she decided with her friends that they would all sign up for the R.A.F. and agreed to meet the following day to volunteer together. When Flora arrived at the town hall, she was the only one who had turned up. Standing outside the building, she had two choices: (1) go back to her friends, listen to all the excuses as to why they didn't go through with it, believe they were all valid reasons and live her life in their shadow or (2) choose what she really felt was the right thing for her, despite having to do it alone.

She chose the latter.

This was someone who lived by her own values and did what she felt was the right thing to do. Had Flora, my gran, not done her own thing, she may never have met my grandpa, and I may never have been born! Thus you have Flora's courageousness to thank for having my book in your hand today...

My gran has always been an inspiring role model and I pass on the above personal story in the hope that you too, take the right action for you. Choose the right thing for you to do, even if you do think you're alone whilst doing. The alternative, is to listen to all the excuses from everyone around you believing they're all valid and live in the shadow of others who reach for their financial success.

A favour please

I wrote this to help you and many others like you to file their tax return with ease and eliminate (or at least reduce!) your money worries. Please help me share this message and if you feel you have learned something from this book, I would be incredibly grateful if you could please write a review on the bookseller's website and tell everyone in your network.

Thank you!

Helen x

Contact me

If you have any questions you wish to ask, please email me at *hello@hmcoaching.co.uk*. Your feedback does matter to me and I will reply as soon I can.

Book Resources and Privacy Notice
To access the resources mentioned throughout the book, please sign up here:
https://www.hmcoaching.co.uk/magicalmixresources

   If you sign up for the free resources, your details will be kept secure and used to send you the resources, annual updates and notifications of any further books I write or online courses I create. You will NOT be added to any other external mailing list, nor sent a million emails... I respect your time and email inbox.

Blogs & Workshops
To be kept informed about the latest workshops I am running or a link to the latest words of wisdom shared via my blog, please sign up by visiting either:

https://www.hmcoaching.co.uk/blog/
Or
https://www.hmcoaching.co.uk/events-workshops/

Social Media Links

If you enjoy social media and wish to see regular updates, please follow me on any of the following:

Twitter: hmfinancecoach
https://twitter.com/hmfinancecoach

Facebook: HM Finance Coaching
https://en-gb.facebook.com/hmcoaching/

Instagram: HM Finance Coaching
https://www.instagram.com/hmfinancecoaching/

LinkedIn: Helen Monaghan
https://uk.linkedin.com/in/helenmonaghanbusinesscoach

Further Useful Resources

Successful Business Minds by Helen Monaghan

12 Steps to Improve Your Cashflow by Helen Monaghan

Become a Warrior Woman: 9 Rules to Sort Your Sh*t by Jen Wilson

The Big Leap by Guy Hendricks

Leap! Ditch Your Job, Start Your Own Business and Set Yourself Free by Ian Sanders

Get your Sh*t Together by Sarah Knight

Manage Your Critic by Sheryl Andrews

The Obstacle is the Way by Ryan Holiday

The Richest Man in Babylon by George S. Clason

Breaking the Habit of Being Yourself by Joe Dispenza

The Power of Your Subconscious Mind by Joseph Murray

You are Awesome: Find your confidence and dare to be brilliant at (almost) anything by Matthew Syed (this is written for children but it's a great reminder that skills only come with practice)

Acknowledgements

All authors have a team behind them and if it weren't for my team this book would never have reached you.

Those at the forefront and who get the brunt of my absence whilst writing a book are Doug and Margaret, followed closely by my family and friends. A massive thank you to all for supporting me and encouraging me to do what I love. Your understanding and acceptance of the passion I have to write is acknowledged. Please know that I'm incredibly grateful for your patience and support.

I would like to acknowledge the role my clients and other business owners in my network play. I am privileged you share the challenges you face and trust me to help you. Additionally, thank you to all the readers of my previous two books; your support is what keeps me writing. I do enjoy writing but knowing someone reads what I've written helps!

To my mentors and mastermind buddies, in no particular order: Saffron, Sian, Alisoun, Kim, Jen, Michelle, Mary, Karen, Sheryl, Avril, Aly, Jill and Lorraine. Thank you for keeping me sane and reminding me to walk my talk when I forget.

Lastly, I would also like to acknowledge the community of indie authors, offline and online, who surround me with their support and encouragement to get the books out of my head and into print. A special thanks in particular to Kim & Sinclair, at Indie Authors World, the 'gang' at the Indie Authors Café each month and Janice Gilbert for her wonderful assistance in editing this book.

About the Author

Helen Monaghan is a Chartered Management Accountant, and a part time student in her final year of a psychology degree with the Open University. She likes challenging social constructs, and believes we can have financial freedom long before our retirement through being mindful.

Passionate about eradicating poverty she moves a little step closer each day to finding out how it could be possible. Her company, HM Finance Coaching Ltd, contributes to helping people with their finances so they can have a life that is devoid (or at least reduced!) of money worries, and her books, she hopes reach everyone who needs them.

If you found this book helpful, please help her reduce poverty by telling everyone about it. Thank you.